Identity Tug of War

Identity Tug of War

Narrating Leadership Awareness of Congregational Identity

PAUL W. LUCAS

WIPF & STOCK · Eugene, Oregon

IDENTITY TUG OF WAR
Narrating Leadership Awareness of Congregational Identity

Copyright © 2025 Paul W. Lucas. All rights reserved. Except for brief quotations in critical publications or reviews, no part of this book may be reproduced in any manner without prior written permission from the publisher. Write: Permissions, Wipf and Stock Publishers, 199 W. 8th Ave., Suite 3, Eugene, OR 97401.

Wipf & Stock
An Imprint of Wipf and Stock Publishers
199 W. 8th Ave., Suite 3
Eugene, OR 97401

www.wipfandstock.com

PAPERBACK ISBN: 979-8-3852-4758-5
HARDCOVER ISBN: 979-8-3852-4759-2
EBOOK ISBN: 979-8-3852-4760-8

VERSION NUMBER 062525

For Payge. You taught me what it means to belong.

Contents

List of Figures | ix
Acknowledgments | xi
List of Abbreviations | xiii
Introduction | xv

CHAPTER 1
Complexifying Congregational Identity | 1

CHAPTER 2
Defining Congregational Identity | 28

CHAPTER 3
Research Scope | 58

CHAPTER 4
Research Data | 83

CHAPTER 5
Conclusion | 132

APPENDIX
Evaluation Tool | 137

Bibliography | 149

List of Figures

Figure 1: Church Attendance Trends for Halton Hills (Estimated) | 22
Figure 2: Trivial-Essential Spectrum | 37
Figure 3: Visualization of Identities | 38
Figure 4: Tug of War | 44
Figure 5: Barrier Circle Diagram | 45
Figure 6: Worship Wars: Divided Identity | 46
Figure 7: TEST: Refugees in Cape Town Churches | 52
Figure 8: TEST: Refugees in Cape Town Church | 54
Figure 9: TEST: Political Moderates in 1990 vs. 2001 AAC | 56
Table 1: Survey Questions | 79
Figure 10: TEST: Women in RAC | 90
Figure 11: TEST: Simple Church in RAC | 97
Figure 12: Survey Results: RAC: Identity Scale: Comparative Summary | 99
Figure 13: TEST: Different Denominational Backgrounds in KAC | 106
Figure 14: Survey Results: KAC: Identity Scale | 109
Figure 15: TEST: English Speakers in KAC | 113
Figure 16: TEST: KAC in Koradai | 116
Figure 17: TEST: Charismatic Beliefs in Archet | 118
Figure 18: TEST Scale: Archet: Theology vs. Mission | 123
Figure 19: Survey Results: Identity Scale: Archet Average vs. Archet Subgroups | 127

Acknowledgments

I will undoubtedly miss a number of people in these acknowledgments. I have an embarrassment of riches in support and am confident that I will leave something out.

Payge, I don't know why you agreed when your husband decided that it would be a great idea to add this to our crazy life. Thank you for allowing me to start and for pushing me to keep going. When I emerged from the writing dungeon and read an excerpt, when I needed to book another multi-day writing retreat, when I felt I couldn't do this, you always were there. You are my muse.

I'd like to thank my three incredible children: CJ, Mia, and Eliza. I must admit that I was, at the beginning of this program, envious of my colleagues who went through this process without young children at home, but I am now so grateful to have had you three along for the ride. You guys truly made this a joy. Thank you for showing a genuine interest in Dad's very boring writing project. Thank you for the hugs and celebrations when I finally finished a chapter.

This book has been adapted out of my dissertation work at McMaster Divinity College's Doctor of Practical Theology program. Thank you to Christopher Land, my doctoral supervisor, for your guidance throughout this work. Thank you for putting up with my esoteric, scattered thoughts and assisting me in piecing them together. I am incredibly thankful for the mentorship you have provided. Thank you also to my second reader, Lee Beach; external reviewer, Jack Barentsen; and chair, Phil Zylla, for all of your advice, encouragement, and guidance.

Thank you to my friend and colleague Francis Pang. I am extremely grateful for your friendship and encouragement. Thank you for being such an incredible support.

Acknowledgments

Thank you to my brother Jack Lucas for your assistance with the survey portion of this research and for providing me with invaluable advice from an expert. Thank you for being available to answer questions at every stage of my academic journey. Thank you also to my other two brothers, Pip and Tim, for always being encouraging and interested in whatever odd interest I am currently obsessing over.

Thank you to my parents for not only believing I could do this when I didn't, but also providing practical help in the form of writing retreat space. Thank you for your encouragement every step of the way and for providing help in whatever way you can.

Thank you to JP Smits for what feels like a lifetime of friendship, and for believing I had something worth saying when I didn't think I did.

Thank you to my church family at Crossings Community Church. Thank you for your prayers, interest, and support throughout this journey.

Thank you to so many friends and family who have shown me love and support through this journey in no particular order: Ruth Johnson, Ken and Lynne Whitton, Esther and Grant Pringle, Robbert Vandergrift, Cas Vandergrift, Kevin Bernie, Ian Trigg, Seán McGuire, Regan Neudorf, Chris and Kerry Wesley, Carolyn Dyer, Davey and Britni Hooper, and the many whom I have failed to mention. Thank you to all the people who have continued to hold us in prayer.

Abbreviations

AAC	Average American Church
C&MA	Christian and Missionary Alliance
IWOGS	Identification with an Organizational Group Scale
KAC	Koradai Alliance Church
LGBTQ	Lesbian, Gay, Bisexual, Transgender, Queer/Questioning
RAC	Riverdale Alliance Church
SIT	Social Identity Theory
TES	Trivial-Essential Spectrum
TEST	Trivial-Essential-Salience Transformation

Introduction

My earliest memories are intertwined with the inside of church buildings, having actively participated in various church and parachurch initiatives such as Sunday School, Good News Club, Awana, summer camp, Vacation Bible School, family camp, and various mid-week church events. Rather than the stereotypical image of children being forced to attend church, I found comfort and familiarity in these communal settings. Perhaps my sense of belonging was influenced by living in a small town, or by the prevalence of church attendance among my school peers, or perhaps I simply have idealized childhood memories. Regardless, the church served as a second home for me, with our family sometimes attending two different churches on the same day. In retrospect, the church served as a safe haven for a sense of belonging during my formative years. Then, during a time of significant upheaval, I suddenly became an outsider in a new school environment. Concurrently, my domestic life was becoming increasingly unstable, and while I would not have considered myself an outsider, the cohesive "unit" of my childhood, flawed as it was, had become fractured. During this period of transition, the church took on an emphasized role as a sanctuary of belonging, particularly within the confines of youth ministry, where I felt the most deeply connected.

RESEARCH PROBLEM

The research problem for this book emerged out of my own practice of Christian leadership. I have for twelve years served in Christian leadership in various roles, primarily in pastoral roles. These include univocational and multivocational roles across a number of settings, primarily within a local church context. The aforementioned personal experience of finding a

Introduction

place of belonging within the church was formative for me in my early development as a practitioner. I did not expect to become a pastor, and when I found myself in such a role, it was only due to what I would describe as divine intervention through the hands of the church. Despite having grown up with the church as a place of safety and belonging—which I must acknowledge is tragically rare—I did not see myself as identifying with those in leadership. When I found myself in such a role, I felt like an outsider among my peers, even though I still felt that I belonged in the church as a whole. Also, the rose-colored lens through which I viewed the church quickly shattered, as I experienced another side of the church I had not seen. I certainly had known that churches had issues, and indeed, in my youth, I was often angered by actions of churches. However, I do not recall losing the sense that I belonged to a church. This changed when I was laid off with little warning during the sickness of my first child and effectively abandoned by the church community I had served the year prior. This also changed in subsequent years as various people expressed to me throughout my time in ministry that my mental disorders are not real, that they are a reflection of my lack of faith, or that they disqualify me from my role. Even still, however, there have been times where I have found deep community. In the midst of all of these changes, the following research question emerged: How do we, as a church, create a place of belonging? Or in more specific terms, how can I, as a church leader, be consciously aware of the individual characteristics of the people who attend my church, of the collective characteristics of my church as a group, and of the ways in which these two things come together in order to create (or prevent) a sense of belonging?

Although my interest in experiences of belonging is a general one, the focus of this book is on church leadership in the context of the Canadian Christian church. To be sure, experiences of congregational identity are not entirely dependent on church leadership, but my immediate concern here is with the leadership practice of developing a conscious self-awareness of communal identity, since leaders act—whether knowingly or unknowingly—as influences on their congregations. Greater awareness of congregational identity can enable leaders to be more effective at shaping communal identity and at bringing their congregations into greater awareness of their communal identity. And together, these things can help leaders to cultivate stronger experiences of belonging in ways that align with the community's stated identity and purpose.

Introduction

DEFINING BELONGING AND AWARENESS

Numerous churches, quite possibly the majority, have as a central objective the aspiration to cultivate a sense of belonging. Yet, an examination of this endeavor reveals a diverse array of interpretations held by churches and their constituents regarding the concept of fostering belonging. To illustrate, one church may posit that an approachable welcome accompanied by coffee, friendly faces, and a contemporary ambiance serves to create a sense of familiarity, enabling individuals to lower their defences upon entering the community. Another congregation may believe that encouraging all members to participate in small and intimate gatherings will foster belonging. Another church may believe that regular fellowship functions that include shared meals allow church members to act as a family and grow in relationship with one another. Another may feel that separating themselves from the world fosters a deep community. The complexities of stimulating belonging stem from a lack of agreement on its provision as well as from the vastly different ways in which belonging can be fostered or hampered.

Barriers to belonging are not always the result of a faith community's lack of kindness or refusal to be welcoming. A church may be concerned that removing entry barriers which are tied to emphasized self-defined identities will change its communal identity to an unacceptable degree. Factors that promote non-member inclusion will inevitably clash with factors that promote the development of a strong in-group identity and, as a result, factors that are "welcoming" can actually militate against a strong sense of belonging among group members.

For this book, belonging will be defined as the feeling or belief of being included within a community such that, as an individual, one functions as part of a wider collective.[1] As a result, the leadership awareness that is in view will be defined as the ability of a leader to self-consciously understand the correlations (or lack thereof) that exist between a congregant's identity and the wider collective (the local church, churches within that community, the wider community), as well as the various forces that influence the

---

1. This definition is formed out of a number of definitions from the field of social psychology, including "the feeling of being accepted and approved by a group or society as a whole" (VandenBos, *APA Dictionary*), "the feeling, belief, and expectation that one fits in the group and has a place there, a feeling of acceptance by the group, and a willingness to sacrifice for the group," (McMillan and Chavis, "Sense of Community," 10) and "the experience of personal involvement in a system or environment so that persons feel themselves to be an integral part of that system or environment" (Hagerty et al., "Sense of Belonging," 172).

strength of these (non-)correlations. In other words, the question is how well pastors can discern the extent to which people within their congregation are operating not solely as individuals but as people who see themselves as belonging to a group.

It is important to note that this definition does not give a binary measure of belonging, and people will vary in their self-assessment of belonging to a certain group. This concept is summarized well by Jack Barentsen, who observes,

> In much of modern life, the dynamics of inclusion and exclusion are highly complex. People may feel included in some groups in some spheres of life but excluded in other groups in other spheres of life. The inclusion and exclusion may also operate in one's sense of belonging to one particular community (of faith), feeling more included along some dimensions and less included along other dimensions.[2]

This contrasts with common rhetoric within Christian circles which portrays someone as either a member of the group or outside of the group, and which fosters a desire to bring people from non-belonging into belonging. While these categories exist, there is a spectrum along which members of religious groups will fall, and the degree of belonging, as will be seen, is not static.

Self-awareness regarding these complexities of communal identity is therefore necessary for effective Christian leadership, and for faithful participation in the mission of God in the world. Self-awareness can be defined as the conscious knowledge and understanding of one's own thoughts, feelings, behaviors, and personal characteristics. It involves the ability to reflect on oneself, recognize patterns, and have a clear perception of one's own identity and impact on others. Self-awareness involves an individual's awareness of their own mental states, including thoughts, emotions, and intentions.[3] It is "the ability to reflect on oneself, to be aware of one's own internal states, desires, beliefs, and actions, and to recognize oneself as the source of those actions and beliefs."[4] It encompasses understanding one's own values, motivations, strengths, weaknesses, and how these factors influence one's behavior. For leaders, the importance of self-awareness extends to communal awareness. Communal self-awareness, therefore,

2. Barentsen, "Apostasy," 72.
3. Duval and Wicklund, *Theory of Objective*, 35.
4. Morin, "Self-Awareness," 36.

involves the conscious knowledge and understanding of both the individual characteristics of the people who make up the group and the collective characteristics of the group. For a leader to be practicing self-awareness regarding experiences of belonging, they need to be operating with a clear perception of the perceived ideal congregational identity of the church, the various collective identities which exist both in and around the church, and the impact of these identities on the various subgroups and individuals in a church community.

OVERVIEW OF RESEARCH

This research develops a deeper understanding of how congregations and church leaders can develop self-awareness of both congregational and subgroup communal identities. This was accomplished through a thick description of identification factors within communities of faith, so as to identify where salient and emphasized communal identities can interplay with factors of belonging, inclusion, and exclusion. An initial survey of four churches led to a subsequent narrative study of three churches. The data from this qualitative research was then presented to church leaders and their feedback was received. This produced a description of factors of belonging in the three communities of faith under study, leveraging both the general surveys and the personal narratives. Included in this description is data concerning leadership self-awareness and reflections concerning the usefulness of these frameworks for church leadership.

This work utilizes Social Identity Theory (SIT) as a theoretical lens of understanding. SIT focuses on how individuals define themselves based on their membership in social groups and how this influences their behavior and attitudes. Coleman Baker provides a succinct summary of SIT as follows:

> Social identity is defined as the "aspects of an individual's self-image that derive from the social categories to which he perceives himself as belonging" (Tajfel 1986: 16). Thus, social identity refers to that part of an individual's sense of identity that comes from belonging to a particular group and is the line of interaction between personal and group identity. Furthermore, social identity "derives from his knowledge of his membership of a group together with

the value and emotional significance attached to the membership" (Tajfel 1982: 63).[5]

SIT theorizes that identity, both personal and communal, is defined through belonging in groups and through the interaction of group and personal identity. As such, SIT provides useful tools for the exploration of congregational identity. The theory of SIT will be explored in detail in chapter 2. It is then employed in the narrative study developed and presented in chapters 3–4. Out of this research an evaluation tool has been produced in the hope that it will help additional congregations and leaders (see appendix 1).

This book explores the challenge for church leaders to understand and practice self-awareness of congregational identity, focusing on the Canadian Christian church context. In the current Canadian context, which is undergoing cultural and demographic changes at a rapid rate, church leaders are having to regularly navigate significant communal shifts. The narrative method and theoretical framework of SIT provide a lens through which Canadian leaders can develop clearer conceptions of communal identity. This can enhance leadership effectiveness and foster communal self-awareness, ultimately leading to healthier guidance and congregational self-awareness.

---

5. Baker, "Social Identity Theory," 130.

CHAPTER 1

Complexifying Congregational Identity

PRACTICAL THEOLOGICAL RESEARCH

Practical Theology

THERE DOES NOT EXIST—to the detriment of theology students—a universally held definition of practical theology. In addition to being understood as an academic discipline, practical theology can be understood as an activity of faith, a method for studying theology, or a curricular area.[1] Practical theology, within this book, refers to a critical reflection on theological practice that impacts current and future practice, often challenging existing assumptions and practices.[2] This critical reflection often brings the practical theologian into conversation with other voices which emerge from practice, interdisciplinary theory, and, of course, theology. This allows practical theology to function as a tool to address the one-way relationship which can emerge between practice and theory.[3]

The aforementioned definition is far from the only widely accepted definition of practical theology. The diverse definitions of practical theology underscore its multidimensional nature.[4] Different definitions bring different focal points into focus, coming together to enable a broad and nuanced understanding of the discipline. One framework, proposed by

1. Miller-McLemore, "Five Misunderstandings," 20.
2. Swinton and Mowat, *Practical Theology*, 23.
3. Veling, *Practical Theology*, 5–6.
4. Miller-McLemore, "Five Misunderstandings," 20.

Osmer, suggests four core tasks and various normative approaches, providing a structured foundation for practical theology.[5] This systematic approach encompasses descriptive-empirical, interpretive, normative, and pragmatic tasks, demonstrating the comprehensive nature of the discipline and its commitment to engaging with diverse perspectives on normatively, such as theological interpretation and ethical reflection.[6] In contrast, David Tracy's definition emphasizes the essential correlation between Christian theory and praxis, highlighting the dynamic interplay between tradition and present reality. Tracy's perspective underscores the importance of interpreting contemporary situations considering Christian beliefs and practices, creating a bridge between the theological framework and the lived experiences of individuals and communities.[7]

Swinton and Mowat's depiction of practical theology emphasizes the lived reality of the church in practice, engaging with the world within the context of God's redemptive actions.[8] Veling adds another layer, framing practical theology as an effort to heal the often one-way division between theory and practice.[9] Cahalan and Nieman offer a structured map that progresses logically from discipleship to discernment, providing a road map for navigating the complex interplay between theory and lived experience.

It is also crucial to draw a distinction between applied theology and practical theology as defined here. As stated by Swinton and Mowat, "in opposition to models that view Practical Theology as applied theology, wherein its task is simply to apply doctrine worked out by the other theological disciplines to practical situations, within this definition, Practical Theology is seen to be a critical discipline which is prepared to challenge accepted assumptions and practices."[10] In other words, practical theology by nature will challenge the status quo and question traditional and current beliefs and practices in order to better understand and serve God's purpose in the world. This critical approach allows for a deeper engagement with the complexities of real-life situations and a more nuanced understanding of how theology can be applied in practical ways. This is not meant to imply that practical theology, as defined in this book, is solely used as a

---

5. Osmer, *Practical Theology*, 4.
6. Osmer, *Practical Theology*, 161.
7. Tracy, "Foundations," 73.
8. Swinton and Mowat, *Practical Theology*, 24.
9. Veling, *Practical Theology*, 5–6.
10. Swinton and Mowat, *Practical Theology*, 23.

deconstructing tool for Christian practice. Indeed, the project of practical theology is often quite the opposite. Practical theology is a dynamic and evolving field that seeks to integrate theological insights with the lived experiences of individuals and communities in order to discern what faithful embodiment of Christ continues to look like.

Miller-McLemore provides an extensive summary of the task of practical theologians:

> Practical theologians assume a number of tasks. They explore the activity of believers through descriptive study and normative assessment of local theologies. They seek to discern common objectives among the ministerial subdisciplines and in the study of theology more generally. They study patterns of integration, formation, and transformation in theological education and vocational development. They seek methods by which students, faculty, and ministers might bridge practice and belief, such as ethnography, narrative theory, case study, and the hermeneutical circle of description, interpretation, and response. They develop theologies of discipleship, ministry, and faith, using secular sources, such as the social sciences and literature, in addition to Scripture, history, and doctrine. In each instance, the development of theory aims to enhance the connective web of theological formation, bridging specific disciplines and ecclesial and educational institutions toward the aim of ministry and the life of faith.[11]

This summary outlines the multifaceted tasks of practical theologians and the task to bridge practice and belief using diverse methods and sources. This is shown in this book, as practice, theology, theory, and method all work together in a connective web of theological formation. This approach underscores the commitment of practical theology to fostering meaningful theological knowledge through critical reflection in a way that arises out of practice and has a transformational impact on theological practice. Out of practical theological reflection, existing assumptions will be questioned and challenged in a manner which can produce new insight and direction to direct future practice, theory, and theology.

---

11. Miller-McLemore, *Christian Theology*, 109.

Practice-Led Research

How does one actually undertake the integration of theology, theory, and practice? The chasm between practice and theory is certainly not exclusive to practical theology. Rather, a concern for bringing theory and practice into conversation with each other is shared across a number of disciplines. While these considerations have been discussed using a wide variety of terms, including reflective practice and practice based research, for the purposes of this book this integration will be called practice-led research.[12]

Practice-led research is an interplay between theory and practice which is primarily concerned with the production of new knowledge which informs practical concerns in a particular field. The focal point of the research should, in practice-led research, be a problem which exists in the researcher's practice. The researcher should have practical experience in the area of their study, and out of their vocational work should emerge a discovery of a problem within the operational field. This will provide the researcher with a hands-on understanding of the cultural atmosphere, the state of an organization, and the results of various approaches towards an issue. The goal is to provide renewed understanding which seeks to address the problem. This may not come in the form of a clear solution—although it is possible for solutions to emerge, what matters is that the work produces a complexified understanding of an issue or even simply a thick description which draws together practice and theory, inviting further reflection.

On the topic of theological practice-led research, Ferguson writes, "Since theology, as understood here, is grounded in faith, it can never be detached from the faith community in which it is developed, nor can the attempt be made to do so. Therefore, a significant aim in developing a practice-led research as a theological method is to establish a working relationship between the triumvirate of faith, intellect, and practice."[13] While the interplay between theory and practice offers many advantages to the

---

12. One aspect that adds to the complexity of defining these terms is that in some works these terms are used interchangeably or to refer to the same type of research, and in other works these terms are brought as contrary terms. All these terms emerge out of a shared desire to bridge practice and theory, but within the development of these various research styles, certain approaches are solidified. Generally, practice-based research is dependent on the development of artifacts. Practice-led research, generally, is concerned with the nature of practice and leads to new knowledge which has operational significance for a practice (Candy, "Practice Based Research," 3). Therefore, the term practice-based research is not used to describe this research.

13. Ferguson, *Practice-Led Theology*, 54.

practical theologian, a number of ethical, practical, and research-based issues emerge when bridging theological practice to theoretical research. Some practitioner-researchers may be able to develop research which is entirely in their own practice and work.[14] However, there are a number of issues which the practical theologian must consider regarding the degree to which their own practice is involved in the research. A potential pitfall of any practice-led research is the increased risk of the bias of the researcher. While other research methods intentionally seek to add degrees of separation between the researcher and the subject of research, practice-led research often brings these closer. Given the personal nature of theological practice, the practical theologian is far from immune to such increased bias. Therefore, the practitioner-researcher functions in a tension between the benefits and costs of bringing one's own personal practice deeper into the research.[15]

In the field of health-care—another discipline where practice-led research features extensively—it is recommended to take a step back and look at the problem within the field from a broader scope: "Once they 'step back' or become dissociated from the object of their practice (process, activity, etc.) which is problematic or 'incomplete' (i.e., it has unknowns which are complex and liable to 'unfold' into further uncertainties); they can proceed to investigate and examine the object as they seek to know it."[16] The usefulness of the research goals emerges from the practical experience working within a field, and the task of practice-led research will develop problems which are complex and whose research will positively benefit practitioners within that field. The stepping back of the practitioner is a major key in avoiding the potential pitfalls of practice-led research by broadening the practice to the field of practice rather than to an individual's context.

In the following two sections, I will "step back" in order to consider the theological ideas and practices that most significantly inform my understanding of the church as a complex collection of interplaying identities (including congregational, subgroup, and personal identities), as well as the actual contexts within which my own experiences of church community have taken place and within which my qualitative research takes place.

---

14. Examples of this are found in the origin of practice-led research, namely artistic studies.

15. Ethical concerns are also an important consideration, as discussed in chapter 3.

16. Fillery-Travis and Robinson, "Making the Familiar Strange," 846.

Chapter 2 will also involve stepping back, utilizing the lens of Social Identity Theory to clarify factors which influence belonging.

PASTORAL AND THEOLOGICAL REFLECTIONS ON CONGREGATIONAL IDENTITY

Balancing Belonging

Churches face numerous complexities when it comes to fostering belonging. They must balance the community's self-defined congregational identity and the subgroup identities of those who are within the system, while also considering outsider perceptions of the community and potential barriers to belonging.[17] Existing members of the church community will also likely leave if they do not feel like they belong anymore. Furthermore, a practice which fosters belonging with one individual or group may hinder belonging with others.

Growing up in Elmira, Ontario, I was surrounded by a significant population of Old Order Mennonites, even though my own family was not a part of that community. Despite not being a member, some important individuals in my life belonged to the Old Order Mennonite community. As an observer, I noticed a unique aspect of this community that provides a poignant example. The Old Order Mennonite community, by intentionally distancing itself from mainstream culture, fosters unity within the church around a shared faith that is deeply rooted in a particular cultural context. This culture involves a unique language, fashion, and a departure from modernity.[18] This culture is developed to be set apart from the surrounding world and to maintain a strong sense of community as the local church. Perhaps one of the most noticeable ways in which this community differs is through their use of horses and buggies. I once had it explained to me by a member of the Mennonite community that the reason that cars are not allowed is that they cause the community to be spread apart geographically. We have seen this to be true in communities accross Canada, with

---

17. Estes ("A Seminarian's Word") provides an insightful outlook of the narration of the identity of outsiders in the local church. Estes explores intergroup bias through the lens of SIT and the justification of practices of exclusion and violence in North American churches.

18. This certainly is also shared by a number of Mennonite and Anabaptist movements. The sole reason for the focus on Old Order Mennonites is simply due to my personal familiarity with this community.

Canadians not nessesarily living, working, and shopping in the same community. This reality is also present in Canadian churches. However, within the Mennonite community, there is lower engagement with outside society. There is a high barrier to belonging, and individuals who leave struggle to remain engaged.[19] This is an example of high degrees of belonging occurring at the cost of raising barriers to belonging. Another example of this occurs in immigrant congregations, a rapidly growing section of the Canadian church. Often, these churches will share a language, a culture, and the journey of immigration. This will, in turn, offer deeply needed relationships for newcomers to Canada. Issues arise among second- and third-generation immigrants, however, who do not share such a strong cultural identification with their parents' native country and language.[20]

We can imagine a weighted scale where on one end of the scale is being open to outsiders and the other end is being a tight-knit community. A lower or "heavier" side indicates this is the stronger pull. It is noteworthy that these are not binary options. If being a tight-knit community is more weighted, this does not mean that a community is completely exclusive to outsiders. Furthermore, this is once again referring to psychological barriers to belonging and identity, not to physical exclusion from gatherings or even intentional exclusion from communal participation. A church can eagerly desire to include outsiders, yet nevertheless be a community where non-members feel extremely out of place. Moreover, depending on why outsiders feel this way, it may be almost impossible for them to imagine ever belonging to the community—and this may have little to do with how the community views itself.

One might react to the above scenario and suggest that the scale needs to move in the opposite direction. In fact, during the narrative interviews in this book, the overwhelming majority of respondents, when asked whether they would see it better to tip the scale in one direction or the other, chose openness to outsiders.[21] A church with the scale tipped all the way the

---

19. Hostetler, *American Mennonites*; Regehr, *Mennonites in Canada, 1939–1970*; Smucker, "Religious Community"; Fretz, *Waterloo Mennonites*.

20. Kwon, *Korean Americans*; Botros, "Religious Identity"; Beattie, "Ethnic Church."

21. These answers may emerge from a sense from respondents that the scale has been tipped too far the other way. I believe the answers did reflect an elevation of importance of the "openness to outsiders" scale above being a close-knit community, save a small number of exceptions. However, I do not want to misconstrue these answers to imply that they believed it should be fully tipped towards being open to outsiders, only that there was a higher value of that end of the scale.

other way would reflect a congregation where there are few initial barriers to becoming part of the community. But such communities also lack intra-group connection on a deeper level. Congregants feel lost in the crowd, as if there is not a significant impact based on whether they do or do not engage within the community.[22] If we return to our definition of belonging—the feeling or belief of being included within a community of faith, such that, as an individual, one functions as part of a wider collective—then we do not see a significant degree of belonging here.

Looked at in this way, a scale tipped towards a tight-knit community will foster belonging for insiders, but create high barriers of belonging for outsiders. A scale tipped in the opposite direction will foster low barriers for a low level of belonging, but a generally lower sense of belonging among congregants. This reflects a tension which churches face when it comes to belonging. As churches, we will say that we wish to be a place to belong, but for whom? Do we want to foster the belonging of existing members? Where are we willing to reduce belonging for our intra-church community in order to allow lower barriers for those currently outside of it? Where might such a reduction result in a community that has no particular identity with which anyone might want to identify?[23]

Holiness and Presence

The complexities that underlay these questions appear also in the biblical motif of holy presence. The idea of holiness, or being "set apart," emerges both in God's relationship to humanity and in those whom God has called to be set apart.[24] In several biblical narratives, the holy presence of God makes one's own sinfulness become salient. God's presence is continually shown to be with Israel in forms such as a burning bush, a fire, a cloud, and dwelling in the Ark of the Covenant. In all these examples, there is

---

22. It is intentional that I use the word *engagement* rather than attendance, because this scenario can occur within regular attendance. Just as exclusion to outsiders should not be thought of as barring people from gatherings, so does lack of engagement within the community not necessarily indicate lack of attendance. This certainly can be a result, but we also may see people who attend ritually but have no significant sense of belonging.

23. There is a tendency among pastors—myself included—to use belonging as a binary descriptor—e.g., someone is an insider or an outsider. As highlighted in defining belonging, this is too simplistic to describe the complexity of belonging within a community of faith.

24. Webster, "Holiness," 249; Gammie, *Holiness in Israel*, 195.

an element of separation which must occur between humanity's sinfulness and the holy presence of God.[25] However, the fullness of the presence of God and humanity come together in the incarnation: God made flesh. This is summarized by Saint Athanasius:

> What was to be done save the renewing of that which was in God's image, so that by it men might once more be able to know Him? But how could this have come to pass save by the presence of the very Image of God, our Lord Jesus Christ? . . . It could not else have taken place had not death and corruption been done away. Whence He took, innatural fitness, a mortal body, that while death might in it be once for all done away, men made after His Image might once more be renewed. None other then was sufficient for this need, save the Image of the Father.[26]

Thus, God's intimate presence with humanity and the holiness of God are met in Christ.[27] However, the presence of God—and by extension the holiness of God—is found through the work of Christ in the Holy Spirit: "But I tell you the truth: it is to your advantage that I am leaving; for if I do not leave, the Helper will not come to you; but if I go, I will send Him to you." (John 16:7 NASB). In this, the presence of God is shown to be within the church, those who are in Christ:

> Consequently, you are no longer foreigners and strangers, but fellow citizens with God's people and also members of his household, built on the foundation of the apostles and prophets, with Christ Jesus himself as the chief cornerstone. In him the whole building is joined together and rises to become a holy temple in the Lord. And in him you too are being built together to become a dwelling in which God lives by his Spirit. (Eph 2:19–21 NIV)

Therefore, the church enters into this tension. We are called as the church to be the presence of God in the world, to be present in the world; yet also, to rid ourselves of that which is not holy.[28] This tension is analogous to the aforementioned tension between the dissolution of differentiation with

---

25. Clements, *God and Temple*, 25–39.

26. Athanasius, *On the Incarnation*, 98.

27. This is an extensive understatement of a tremendous theological discussion, and there is much that should be said and has been said on this topic. However, this section is not intended to be an exhaustive theological overview of these topics, but rather reflecting pastorally on these theological principles.

28. Esler, "Social Identity," 54–55; Toney, "Strong and Weak," 34–35; Horrell, "Solidarity and Difference," 66–67.

outsiders and the development of internal community. The church balances lowering the differentiation between itself and outsiders and also fostering deep belonging within the community, emerging from a differentiated collective identity of the church.

These tensions were grappled with in the early Christian church, and examples of this are found in the Pauline epistles. Rosell Nebreda's study of the Philippian hymn suggests a transformation of the Christ-following community's identity, moving away from ethnic and social distinctions, and giving rise to a new, superordinate collective identity.[29] On the issue of food, Paul writes to the church in Rome, "The one who eats everything must not treat with contempt the one who does not, and the one who does not eat everything must not judge the one who does, for God has accepted them" (Rom 14:3 NIV). In this passage, Paul recognizes the need to lower differentiation within intergroup identities of those who feel comfortable eating these foods and those who do not.[30] In this situation, the comfort is likely tied to religious backgrounds prior to becoming members of a Christian community. However, Paul also recognizes that in some situations, food may generate social tensions involving conflicting social identities, saying, "If an unbeliever invites you to a meal and you want to go, eat whatever is put before you without raising questions of conscience. But if someone says to you, 'This has been offered in sacrifice,' then do not eat it, both for the sake of the one who told you and for the sake of conscience" (1 Cor 10:27–28 NIV). Moreover, earlier in 1 Corinthians, we read Paul's response to an issue of sexual immorality, with instructions to not associate with a member who has been sleeping with the wife of his father (1 Cor 5:9–11). Here, Paul creates clear divisions and promotes an exclusionary practice.[31] So, on the issue of sexual immorality within the church, there was no way this practice could, according to Paul, be acceptable in any church. Yet Paul affirmed the Christian personal identity of believers as one that must intentionally embrace and incorporate a diverse array of social identities.[32]

The Corinthian community grappled with confusion over personal and subgroup identity positions, revealing the ongoing process of redefinition and complexification. Paul addresses various social divisions, emphasizing the need for a unified, Christ-centered identity that transcends worldly

---

29. Nebreda, *Christ Identity*.
30. Esler, "Social Identity," 54.
31. Tucker, *"Remain in Your Calling,"* 188.
32. May, "Body," 109; Tucker, *"Remain in Your Calling,"* 229.

distinctions. Darlene Seal shows how Paul expresses a twofold worry about how the Corinthian community is perceived by outsiders and the need to differentiate them from external groups.[33] His letters to Corinth lack references to tension between the church community and the surrounding community such as we find in other letters (e.g., 1 Thessalonians). This suggests, to some, that Paul views the Corinthian community as under-differentiated from the wider culture.[34] The intragroup relationships among the Corinthians are similarly problematic, revealing behavioral evidence of aversion and tension within the church community. Specific issues such as idol food consumption become focal points of conflict within the community.[35] Seal emphasizes Paul's attempts to address these conflicts by drawing attention to commonalities among group members in order to foster unity and mitigate intragroup aversion.[36] Thus, the New Testament itself gives us a great illustration of how important it is for leaders to shape communal identity carefully. Paul needed to clarify in-group/out-group distinctions so as to define the collective identity of the Corinthian community, enabling in-group diversity wherever possible while simultaneously maximizing holiness but minimizing in-group division and infighting.

What Defines the Church?

Belonging issues are frequently present but unnoticed, resulting in barriers to belonging that are not integral to the community's self-conscious identity.[37] Some churches may not reflect deeply about how they foster or hinder belonging, and may feel this is unimportant. Although a leader may believe that the community's "official" vision statement shapes its congregational identity, other members of the congregation or members of the community may see the group's identity from a completely different perspective. An example of low self-awareness of barriers to belonging is found in a 2018 study which utilized SIT and microaggressions literature to describe negative interactions and to expose processes which marginalize church members and cause disaffection with the church. This study showed that despite

---

33. Seal, "These Things," 152–54.
34. Ho, "Cleanse Out the Old Leaven," 257–57; Esler, "Keeping It in the Family," 145–60.
35. Fee, "Εἰδωλόθυτα Once Again," 193–95; Horrell, *Solidarity*, 166–82.
36. Seal, "These Things," 152–54.
37. Allen et al., "Belonging."

an explicitly inclusive mission espoused by the church being studied, micro aggressions were occurring unknowingly in the church. Responsibility for reparation was left with the targets of these microaggressions, the existence of microaggressions was denied by members of the congregation, and the overall result was a sense of rejection resulting from marginalization.[38] Similarly, a small and close-knit community may be deeply meaningful and produce spiritual growth, but it may appear closed off and unwelcoming to outsiders.[39]

The question "What does it mean to be the church?" will get many different responses depending on background, denomination, culture, history, theology, and more.[40] This is further complicated by the fact that these categories are concerned with what we ought to be, not what we are. And it has been my observation that in the world of church leadership we operate with past centric or future centric language, rarely entering into the present tense. The question of "who are we" as a church often looks to the past, future, and sometimes both. The past includes a shared origin story, theological distinctions, and key identities created during the formation of a community. The future aspects include visions, trends in culture, plans, and goals. Furthermore, even within these categories, people may not be able to accurately identify the manner in which these factors arose, or how they actually contribute to ongoing experiences. For example, a theological distinction may have been key in a church's formation, especially if a church was born out of a split, but what role does that distinction continue to play after a number of years or even decades have passed? For some individuals, the theological distinctive may be central to their sense of communal identity, whereas for others it may be unnoticeable or even unknown. Similarly, when assessing future vision, there may or may not be a generally accepted future vision of the church.[41] Or, even if there is such a vision, it may be so

---

38. Dowdle, "Disaffection."

39. Wuthnow, "Community Spirit."

40. The topic of Christian identity is far reaching, and while the scope of this research focuses on self-awareness of congregational identity, there have been many theological works relating to the emergence of Christian identity. For example, see Hauerwas, *Character*; Capps, *Decades of Life*; Roberts, *Spiritual Emotions*; Conradie, *Christian Identity*.

41. Gill ("The Cultural Paradigm") explores the connection between a decline in religious belonging and a decline in religious belief, arguing for a cultural paradigm as a framework to look at the transmission of belief and the role of socialization. He first unpacks three alternate paradigms of secularization, persistence, and separation, and then unpacks his cultural paradigm which looks at a causal relationship between belonging and belief. His book *Changing Worlds* also provides an outlook on trends within the

radically disconnected from the present reality of the community that it is difficult to imagine how the future congregational identity might arise from the present one. In such moments, communities often undergo significant changes in membership, as individuals reevaluate their current sense of belonging in light of what is essentially an imagined identity. Leaders need to be aware that this is happening, so they need to understand the present reality of the community in relation to its past and (ideal) future.

The self-identity of communities is often self-referenced by the community through collective narrative formation, that is, the shared narrative of a group. A scriptural motif which shows this is the Exodus narrative, which helps to demonstrate a manner in which collective identity forms through narrative. The example of the Exodus narrative with the people of Israel helps us to develop a broader understanding of the enduring nature of shared narratives in shaping the collective identity of ecclesiastical bodies over time. Stargel utilizes SIT to provide a practical way to understand identity formation within the Exodus narrative, solidifying the communal identity of the Israelite community through shared experiences.[42] The collective experiences, challenges, and successes contribute to the complex construction of communal identity in both the Exodus narrative and in ancient Israel. This underscores the lasting influence of the narrative, highlighting its appropriation by succeeding generations. The journey of many churches mirrors that of ancient Israel, characterized by continuous rehearsal and participation in its narrative.[43] Stargel's research encourages a broad ecclesiastical recognition of the ongoing role of shared stories in defining collective identity in Christ. The successive appropriation of the narrative underscores the need for active engagement and participation in the communal narrative, ensuring its sustained relevance and influence on ecclesiastical identity at large.[44]

Israel's scriptural history sees segmentation, division, alliances, and separation shape its landscape. These intergroup and intragroup identities include but certainly are not limited to Benjaminite versus Judean identity

---

wider culture and community of faith, church growth and decline, and changes within theological education.

42. Stargel, *Construction of Exodus Identity*.

43. A recent study which has explored the nuances of this in an African context is Du Toit, "Rethinking Identity Theory."

44. Stargel, *Construction of Exodus Identity*.

in Jeremiah,[45] Judean versus Samaritan identity,[46] Moabite versus Israelite identity,[47] and the identity of exiled Judea.[48] In the same way, we see segmentation, division, alliances, and separation shape the Christian church's identity through denominational, theological, ecclesiastical, cultural, and gender-based divisions, among others. As with Israel, the Christian church represents a structure that is not totally united yet also not totally divided. We learn from social psychology that human beings are inherently communal, yet these communities often form out of opposition. Often, communities are built around the shared social grouping of not being the "other." One study that shows this same process occurring in faith groups is Herriot, *Religious Fundamentalism*. This book explores through SIT why fundamentalist groups self-identify as an in-group fighting against various out-groups, and why the psychological needs for self-esteem and meaning motivate these groups.[49] This plays a significant role in the interaction of church and culture, and in particular within a culture where there is a move away from Christianity being a primary voice in the public arena. There are communities which will choose to "other" the wider culture, therefore growing a shared congregational identity in not being the world. Others may reject traditional forms of Christianity or what is seen as the primary way certain faith is expressed in the public arena, and again form communities with the shared congregational identity of not being similar to what they have seen in Christianity. This is quite common in the formation of Christian denominations which are created out of a split. While theological disagreements may be at the center of the actual split, the subsequent formation of the subgroups (i.e., new churches) may have quite salient identities around being different than the group which they were previously a part of.[50]

45. Crabtree, "Prophet."
46. Esler, "Conflict," 329.
47. Diamant, "Group Identity."
48. Sapolu, "Reconciling Identities"; Cook, "Social Identity."

49. Herriot's suggestion is to avoid treating fundamentalism as an enemy to be defeated—which will only enhance the out-group narrative—but to manage these conflicts in a psychologically sensitive manner.

50. We see an effort to redefine the distinctions in the Acts narrative. In this, the distinction was between Judean and non-Judean Christ followers. Baker (*Identity*) shows that this involves positioning Peter and Paul as representative figures contributing to a shared overarching Christian identity. Peter and Paul, in this view, act as prototypes, forming a collective in-group identity that goes beyond ethnic and cultural differences.

Importantly, this approach accommodates the coexistence of subgroup identities within the broader Christian identity framework. Identity formation is occurring within the boundaries of church and community, churches interacting with other churches, and within the intragroup dynamics within a church's congregational identity. These identities are not reducible to a single, universal definition of what the church is, despite the desire of church leaders for a simple and clear definition. Thus, we are not in this book focusing on the theological element of ecclesiology, which refers more to the idealized past and future (and to be clear, is an essential topic for practical theological research), but rather the complex reality of church communities and the perception, experience, and interaction of the various aforementioned subgroups. Put simply, I am interested to see how we, as the church, practice presence and holiness within all the messiness of group identity.

Barriers to Belonging

Social Identity Theory provides a framework for understanding how communities form by "othering" other communities. This does not sound appealing as a church quality—and, to be clear, it has often resulted in intense discrimination, bigotry, and abuse within churches—but it must also be broadened to understand how barriers appear in numerous ways in congregational identity. It is critical for church leaders to identify these barriers to belonging and to evaluate them in light of communal identity. The goal of eliminating all exclusionary practices is impossible and illogical. To belong to a community, one must be able to perceive a difference between that community and other possible communities. It is the task of leaders, then, to help people to perceive the "right" differences.

A second example can be observed when inclusion would transform a community identity in such a way that the church would no longer be unified around essential shared identities. In such instances, the church may decide to exclude people or organizations who do not share its essential principles and ideals. For example, if an atheist is unhappy with teaching about God in a church, the church is unlikely to adjust their views to allow for atheists to feel a strong sense of belonging. However, exclusive practices extend beyond theological stances. A church might have liturgical or aesthetic practices that some individuals see as detracting from their sense of belonging. Should these be considered an essential part of the community's identity? The church leader faces the question "What changes will make us lose our identity (including personal, subgroup, and congregational), and what changes will help us to redefine our identity in a more invitational manner?" The answers are highly complex, as will be explored, but asking such questions is a step toward self-awareness.

The acceptance of barriers to belonging, and by extension, exclusionary identities, may seem to be a process contrary to the role of the church. Indeed, many churches express a strong desire to be open to all regardless of differences. However, it is important to address this with a clear definition of these terms. Identities which would be defined here as exclusionary are shaped by practices, beliefs, or traits that make it harder for a particular group of people to experience a sense of belonging. Identities which would be defined as inclusionary are defined here as practices which contribute to a positive sense of belonging for a particular subset of individuals.[51] Yet belonging, as a facet of human psychology, is by its very nature dependent on the perception of alternative, non-overlapping social identities. The intersectionality of inclusionary and exclusionary parameters is thus a key factor in eliminating *unnecessary* barriers to belonging within communities of faith.

Discerning Identity

Within the Christian church, current social identities need to be evaluated internally in order to act as a community acting in embodied faithfulness to God.[52] This will involve a careful and deliberate process by which systems are observed and understood through their various parts. An analogy can be made from a wide variety of settings, but from personal interest I will make an analogy from car repairs. When repairing a vehicle, it is important to carefully take off each piece of the vehicle in order to be able to reconstruct the vehicle when the issue is resolved. However, often when dealing with older vehicles, rusted parts can prevent the careful process and

---

51. For the sake of clarity, it is important to highlight that this definition ties inclusion and exclusion to a particular set of individuals, often with the result of the respective opposite; that is, an inclusionary practice for one subgroup is exclusionary for another. This will be explored in greater detail, but it is essential to note the difference between this type of categorization and a categorization which would have practices which are universally inclusionary and universally exclusionary.

52. Internal evaluation refers here to evaluating the social identities which are internal to the community, not necessarily that evaluation is done by internal members.

parts need to be forced off. The process of complexification helps to identify problems along the way so that during the reconstruction process rusted parts can be either repaired, replaced, or a solution applied to avoid seizing in the future. In this analogy, the parts of the car refer to the shared identities found in social groupings. As leaders seek to discern the communal identity of a particular denomination or congregation, other shared identities may need to be evaluated, eliminated, or replaced in order to support the continuation of the shared Christian identity. This book particularly focuses on developing awareness of communal identity in order to allow this type of revaluation to occur.

A microcosm of subgroup identity redefinition can be shown scripturally through the experiences of Ruth, a Moabite woman, and Naomi, her Israelite mother-in-law. The narrative transcends ethnic and social boundaries, emphasizing the importance of individual choices in shaping communal identity and highlighting the transformative power of loyalty and selflessness. According to Peter Lau, Ruth's story depicts a significant transformation in her personal identity, from Moabite outsider to integrated member of Israelite society. Despite her assimilation, there is a tension between her foreign origins and her newfound familiarity within the in-group. Ruth's interactions with key characters, Boaz and Naomi, are crucial in this identity shift, highlighting the interdependence inherent in ancient Israel's relational collectivist culture. Her personal characteristics, particularly her initiative, play an important role in shaping her personal and group identity, serving as an implicit example for readers. The example of Ruth contributes to a better understanding of the complex interplay between group identity and ethics by demonstrating how one's choices and actions can influence and transform one's identity, indicating a bilateral relationship between identity and ethics.[53] The identity formation of congregational bodies is a place of exchange between collective and individual identities. This is expressed in a recent study on identity formation in Christians through baptism: "The identity-forming recognition grounded solely on one's status in Christ cuts two ways. It affirms and elevates those who previously were without status and recognition but will challenge the identity of new believers if their self-concept is grounded in some creaturely or cultural standard."[54] This exchange can function as a place of empowerment

---

53. Lau, *Identity*.
54. O'Neil, "Role of Baptism," 15.

to voices which would normally be put at the margins, and can also function as a place where power dynamics reduce dissenting voices.

The practice of self-awareness of communal identity and belonging brings about a complex and multifaceted picture of the various aspects which will contribute in these areas, theological convictions which will push or pull in certain directions, and power structures which may affect or influence these realities. Pastors need to listen to congregational stories in a way that crystallizes identity, creates a coherent history, and generates congregational renewal. Individual perspectives are merged into a congregation's character which is used as a means of communal self-identification. These stories can then be shaped into a narrative that church members can claim as their church's story.[55] Furthermore, the examination of self-awareness of communal identity and belonging also reveals the importance of cultural and historical contexts in shaping these aspects. Additionally, it highlights the significance of individual agency and personal experiences in navigating and negotiating these complex dynamics. According to Swinton and Mowat, situations are complex entities which contain values, meanings, and power dynamics which are hidden.[56] They write, "The task of the practical theologian is to excavate particular situations and to explore the nature and faithfulness of the practices that occur within them."[57] Therefore, within communities of faith, current congregational identity may need to be complexified to embody faithfulness.

I will conclude this discussion with a scriptural example of this complexification from the Gospel of Mark. The account in Mark 10:35–45 presents a paradigm shift that Jesus presents to his disciples in order to clarify their group identity. Justin Dewell analyzes the disciples' lack of self-categorization, specifically focusing on James and John's desire for power despite Jesus' teachings.[58] According to Dewell, the conflict in Mark's narrative reflects the disciples' failure to exhibit Jesus' communicated norms, potentially leading to an incorrect group identity. The identification of the "rulers of the Gentiles" functions as an out-group, contrasting their norm of power with Jesus' in-group norm of service. Jesus challenges the disciples' preconceptions, urging them to redefine their group and personal identities

---

55. Hopewell, *Congregation*, 55–56.
56. Swinton and Mowat, *Practical Theology*, 15.
57. Swinton and Mowat, *Practical Theology*, 15.
58 Dewell, "Known as Servants."

through servanthood.[59] This process of complexifying social identity, both in this scriptural narrative and in the modern church, involves recognizing and understanding the various layers and nuances that contribute to the identities which make up a community of faith. It requires delving deeper into the hidden values, meanings, and power dynamics that shape individuals' experiences and actions within these communities. By doing so, the practical theologian can help uncover the complexities inherent in social identity and guide congregations towards embodying faithfulness.[60] Jesus prays for his disciples in this passage which further shows this pattern of shifting identities in a different manner than the aforementioned Mark passage:

> I have revealed you to those whom you gave me out of the world. They were yours; you gave them to me and they have obeyed your word. . . . I have given them your word and the world has hated them, for they are not of the world any more than I am of the world. My prayer is not that you take them out of the world but that you protect them from the evil one. They are not of the world, even as I am not of it. (John 17:6, 14–16)

In this, we see the bringing of his disciples into himself, even as there is a distancing from the world, yet also a presence within the world. In the Mark passage, differentiation occurs between the rulers of the gentiles and the disciples, and similarly here, differentiation occurs between the disciples and the world. There is much more that can and has been said about this passage, but the purpose of referencing it here is the reflection of Jesus' identities within his own mind which he is shaping in his disciples. In this passage, we see the bringing of Christ's disciples into holiness and presence in the world. The prayer then turns to all who will come to believe through them: "I have given them the glory that you gave me, that they may be one

---

59. Singfiel ("When Servant Leaders") reviews servant and laissez-faire leadership theories and proposes that SIT can explain how leaders are influenced by social identity to self-identify as servants without exercising the characteristics of servant leadership.

60. According to Andrew Dunlop, "Complexity is a necessity in theological reflection—to capture the reality of the situation, and also to do justice to any response . . . good theological reflection is not a simplifying process leading to a clear action, but a complexifying process based on influences from practice and theology" (Dunlop, "Four Voices Theology," 304). Katherine Turpin also writes, "Careful practical theology attends to the particularity of both the context that produced the elements of the tradition that we are engaging and the complexity of the local context we are putting into dialogue with it and decides whether there is enough of a translation possible for a constructive conversation to take place" (quoted in Mercer and Miller-McLemore, *Conundrums*, 264).

as we are one—in them and you in me—so that they may be brought to complete unity. Then the world will know that you sent me and have loved them even as you have loved me" (John 17:22–23). This passage shows an image of Christ praying for the disciples and future church to have a connection that is one, in the same manner that Jesus is one with the Father. This is not to imply the dissolution of personal identities, as Christ and the Father retain personal identities in this description, but rather the oneness which Christ and the Father share. This mystery is intertwined with the goal of complexifying communal identity.

By engaging in the process of complexification, congregations can gain a better understanding of the intricate dynamics at play within their own community. This exploration allows for a more nuanced and thoughtful approach to the practices and beliefs that shape their collective identity. It is imperative for the Christian church to undertake an internal evaluation of current social identities to foster a community grounded in embodied faithfulness to God. This necessitates a meticulous and intentional examination of existing systems, with a focus on understanding their components rather than advocating for their destruction. Through this process, the church can strive towards greater cohesion and alignment with its principles, ultimately fulfilling its mission in the world while working towards being a holy presence.

Shifts in Identity and the Canadian Church

Chapter 3 will explore the context of individual churches in more detail, but it is equally important to explore the general context in which I myself as a practitioner operate and in which the churches being researched find themselves. I serve currently as the pastor at a small church in a small Canadian town. This church is part of The Alliance Canada denomination, also known as The Christian and Missionary Alliance in Canada or the C&MA. My role reflects an increasing trend, in that my primary source of income is not from the church, but from elsewhere. This trend is referred to as multivocational ministry, and it is a growing reality within churches. In our context, it seems to be functioning, and is one of many adaptations which will likely be seen increasingly as the Canadian church context continues to shift. I have also seen many shifts in the role which the church plays within wider society. There are too many shifts to explore here, but one important shift is the shift in Canadian society to become increasingly post-Christian.

In 2001, Halton Hills was made up of 80.9 percent Christian, 18 percent no religion, and the remaining 1.1 percent made up of non-Christian religions. In 2021, this area was 61.6 percent Christian, 32.2 percent no religion, and 6.4 percent non-Christian religions. Thus, the percentage change in religious affiliation in Halton Hills during this period is -19.5 Christian, +14.2 non-religious, and +5.5 other religions. Halton Hills follows national trends with under 5 percent difference of percentage changes when compared to the national percentage changes (-24.2 Christian, +18.6 non-religious, and +5.4 other religion).[61]

We see in the above data that Halton Hills is very aligned with the trends across Canada when it comes to religious affiliation: a drop in Christian affiliation, rise in no affiliation, and small rise in non-Christian religious affiliation. Affiliation, due to its inclusion in the regular Canadian census, is the most accessible data to provide comparisons, but it also does not tell the full picture. Religious affiliation can mean radically different things to different people. For example, those who identify as Christian may not be involved in any church, but may have had family affiliation. Furthermore, identification with a denomination does not mean that one is involved in a community of faith. Figure 1 includes an estimation of monthly attendees based on denomination, weighted with data from a 2019 STATSCAN report on religiosity.[62]

---

61. Clark, "Pockets of Belief"; Cornelissen, "Religiosity in Canada"; "2001 Community Profiles"; "Profile Table."

62. Clark, "Pockets of Belief"; Cornelissen, "Religiosity in Canada"; "2001 Community Profiles"; "Profile Table."

Growth Change

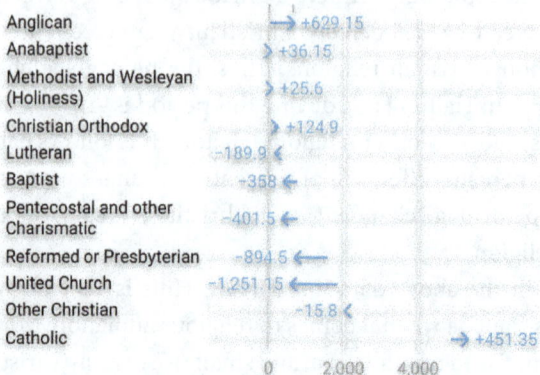

Estimated Monthly Attendance (Halton Hills)

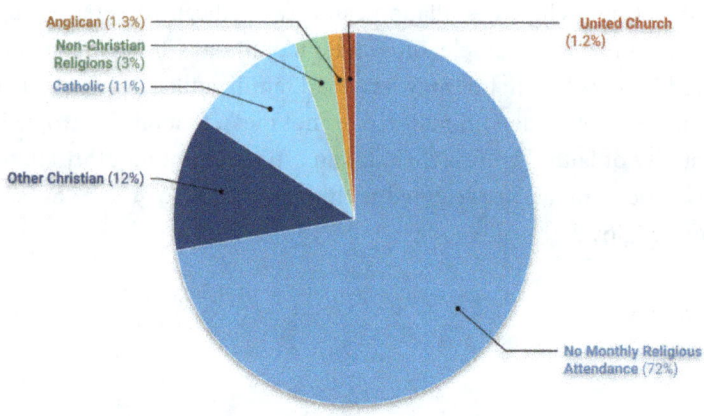

Figure 1: Church Attendance Trends for Halton Hills (Estimated)

We see here a general movement—with the exception of some growth for Anglicans, Christian Orthodox, and Catholics—for lower average church affiliation based on an average of monthly attendance. Both the trends in religious affiliation and in church attendance reveal the overall trend towards a decline in Christianity. While the extent of these trends will vary across Canada, the trend is clearly towards an overall decline in Christian church attendance.[63] A demonstration of this is shown in the

---

63. This is an estimation as the data is developed through weighing religious affiliation with religiosity data on religious service attendance. However, as there is a very high similarity between the trends of the Canadian landscape and Halton Hills, and as the

estimation of religious service attendance that occurs at least once a month. In Halton Hills, 72 percent do not attend a religious service once a month or more, and 3 percent do so at a non-Christian religious service.[64] Out of this data, we can imagine the average Halton Hill resident by four groups of people, identified as blue, purple, pink, and green.[65] The blue and purple group identify as Christian, the green group identifies as non religious, and the pink group is made up of people who identify as either a non-Christian religion or non-religious.

In Halton Hills, only the blue group is regularly involved in church. We used to see more purple group members, but they seem to be less and less. The green and pink groups are becoming much larger. In the past, a pastor who was working in this area might have, while walking around their neighborhood, workplace, or school, seen many blue and purple group members. The primary group identity of being Christian may have been shared by the majority of Canadian society and culture. This is no longer the case. Previously in Canada, a Canadian church would have existed in a society surrounded by people with similar religious identities on average, in contrast to the experience of the church today.

In the past, a lack of differentiation between church and society caused "Christian" identity to have low salience. In contrast, those who are a part of a church community in the present have a very salient religious

---

variance of the religiosity data from the affiliation data is two years, there is good reason to believe this chart accurately reflects the local population distribution of monthly religious service attendance. Adjustments from affiliation data are from Canadian data from 2019 on average weekly attendance by denomination. As there was limited data available for denominational-based attendance rates near 2001, the data reflects an adjustment of the 2021 numbers multiplied by the total change in Canadian Christian monthly attendance from 2001 to 2019.

64. Regular attendance is defined differently within different groups; however, the religiosity data comes not from tracking attendance but from self-reporting. Therefore, this data is less reflective of actual attendance patterns and more reflective of how individuals would report their attendance. This creates a strength of the religiosity data, as attendance can be affected by a number of factors, but self-reporting adds an aspect of self-understanding which is relevant to religious identification with a church. In other words, I am more interested in whether someone sees themselves as regularly attending a church than the actual amount of times per year they attend it.

65. Halton Hills is used as an example due to its proximity to national trends and association with my own practice. The context of this work is not solely Halton Hills but rather the wider Canadian church. Within different geographic or demographic subgroups, the exact makeup of religious affiliation and attendance will shift, but trends remain consistent.

identity.⁶⁶ However, there is another factor that is equally important. One clear oversimplification of this diagram is the amalgamation of "Christian" identity across denominations. In contrast, denominational identity can vary in importance. In the past, differences between denominational identities were very salient, whereas these differences are now being overshadowed by the greater differences that exist between Christians and others in Canadian society.

This second factor can be seen in a study done on the Free Church denomination in Europe through the lens of SIT. Ecclesiological and missiological difficulties of denominations—which in this study was the Free Church in Europe—may be due to the fading of the relevant identity-forming other, namely other Christian groups.⁶⁷ This article suggests that a shift needs to take place in denominational identity through forming identity through other means than opposition to other Christian groups. Using the illustration of colors, we could imagine the denominations being different shades of blue. Thus, within the wider group of blue, we have subgroups of indigo, navy, sapphire, etc.

The historic Canadian church, similar to the aforementioned study, had greater degree of differentiation between denominational groups than today. One of the most salient divides was the Catholic and Protestant divide amongst settlers which included differentiation based on language and culture, as well as religion. This is also found in the relationship between denominational affiliation and country of origin. For example, the descendants of Scottish immigrants tended to remain in Presbyterian churches, the descendants of Dutch immigrants tended to remain in Reform churches, English descendants with Anglican churches, etc.⁶⁸ Catholic affiliation was

---

66. Salient identities will be explored in more detail in the next chapter.

67. Bartholomä, "Ecclesiological Self."

68. An interesting difference between current immigration is that while ethnic-centric churches are becoming increasingly common, these tend to exist across denominations. For example, if a Scot immigrant wanted to worship with other Scots a century ago, they likely would have to remain in the Presbyterian denomination. However, a Korean or Vietnamese immigrant today can find a church within their language and culture across denominations. So, although salient subgroup identities will be present within immigrant communities, this does not increase degree of denominational affiliation as it did in the past. Admittedly, geographic limitations will affect the choice of denomination—there may only be one church of a particular ethnicity in the area—and there are likely exceptions based on percentage of denominational affiliation based on country of origin. However, this trend remains true, as those within the denomination will not be exclusive to a particular place of origin.

similar, with the difference of a plurality of ethnicities or country of origin. For example, both Italian and Irish immigrants tended to be Catholic. As the differentiation increases between Christian identity and the wider Canadian identity, differentiation will likely decrease between denominations. This does not mean that denominational divides necessarily decrease, but rather the differentiation between denominations becomes less salient than other, more salient differences. In other words, the different shades of blue become less noticeable when the blue group is surrounded by other colors.

A post-Christendom society can be defined as a society in which the Christian church at one point held a position of power and authority and no longer holds the power. In *The Church in Exile*, this reality is defined as follows:

> While the church once helped define various forms of empire in the Western world, its influence has abated, and there is within contemporary culture a deconstruction of former beliefs, patterns of life and conventions that defined the world for many generations but no longer do. . . . In the post-Christian revolution, it is fair to say that the church is one of those former power brokers who once enjoyed a place of influence at the cultural table but has been chased away from its place of privilege and is now seeking to find where it belongs amid the ever-changing dynamics of contemporary culture.[69]

As mentioned above, there is a growing trend within my own practice and Canada as a whole towards a decline in the affiliation and involvement within faith groups. This belief in the decreasing influence of Christianity is widely-held, with 64 percent of Canadians reporting agreement that this decrease is occurring.[70] As such, the nature of identity formation becomes ever-increasingly important as we examine how we will form our group and personal identities. Canadian clergy can no longer act as if Canada has a predominately Christian culture as the Christian church no longer occupies a prominent space in the Canadian landscape.[71] In a multicultural, post-Christendom context in which churches are struggling to navigate declining involvement, it is vital that churches reflect carefully on the nature of social identity and the many different factors that can foster or hinder belonging. It is a common occurrence to hear those who leave a church

---

69. Beach, *Church in Exile*, 50.
70. Lipka, "5 Facts."
71. Clarke and Macdonald, *Leaving Christianity*, 197.

community saying that they did not feel they belonged there, or to hear that they found a new community in which they felt they belonged. It is important to help church leaders to reflect carefully on this reality and to consider how their community's identity is formed and shaped, if they wish to create a place where people can potentially find a place of belonging. This will involve, in theory, decreasing unnecessary differentiation between group identity (i.e., those within and outside the church) and a shift in intragroup identity towards essential identities and away from differentiating trivial identities. In practice, this can be very difficult. However, self-awareness of communal identity can help to determine where these factors of differentiation exist and where they might be increased or decreased. In a recent study on applying social identity to pastoral leadership, Jack Barentsen writes,

> While the identity of the church is often considered a divine gift, it is equally a call to socio-religious construction in a particular context and with a particular group of people. This requires the ability to not only interpret Christian sources, but also the social and religious phenomena of our society. These interpretations, in turn, serve to position the church in a credible fashion in its society as well as to position the leader as embodiment and model of the beliefs and values of the church's identity. A pastoral leader, then, is not simply an interpretive guide, but embodies these interpretations in his or her interactions within and outside of the community in a manner that makes him or her a community model or prototype for the current (or changing) vision of the church's identity.[72]

Each congregation needs to consider its group identity and to explore whether barriers to belonging are the result of factors integral to creating and sustaining the group's essential identity or the result of unnecessary and potentially unrecognized factors that are perhaps reducing in-group belong and/or hindering the inclusion of desired newcomers.

CONCLUDING REFLECTIONS

By considering Christian identity through the lens of social identity, we will see a more explicit and comprehensive consideration of significant factors within organized gatherings that can foster or hinder the formation of deep community and a sense of belonging among a community's current

---

72. Barentsen, "Church Leadership," 78.

or potential future members. Through an examination of biblical stories like the Exodus, Ruth, Paul's epistles, and the teachings of Jesus, we see the importance of negotiating and redefining communal identities. Whether ancient Israel or contemporary faith communities, the acknowledgment of out-groups, the formation of subgroups, and the role of differentiation underscore the continual process of reshaping communal identity. These scriptural and modern narratives deepen our understanding of how the interplay between shifting identity and shared stories shapes the collective identity of ecclesiastical bodies across different eras, revealing the enduring relevance of these themes within religious communities.

The Canadian church cannot look to the past as the source of our identity. Our identity is constantly shifting, and a stagnant community can quickly turn toxic. We also must not be arrogant enough to assume that our current identity is close to our idealized goals, or that there is a clear path towards those goals from the standpoint of the present. The complexity of social identity should give us pause, yet even salient identities are not unmovable. Perhaps a richer, holy presence of the church emerges out of the humility of allowing the shifting of identities. When repairing a car, one cannot just leave the parts off, and ecclesiological deconstruction cannot be an end in itself. There will be parts which will be returned to where they were, there will be parts which will be discarded, and there will be parts which need alterations. As a result, the reconstruction perhaps may more deeply reflect in that time the presence of the God who out of love created humanity and for love died and rose again so that we could be one as He and the Father are one. In the Canadian church, this involves a dramatic and at times painful redefining of what it means to be a holy presence in Canada.

Chapter 2

Defining Congregational Identity

The themes of belonging and identity are pervasive in human behavior and psychology. Indeed, these issues can even become relevant during the writing of an academic work. For instance, many individuals who undertake a dissertation, myself included, begin to suffer what is known as imposter syndrome. Imposter syndrome is the feeling that surrounding individuals belong in a certain circumstance—unlike oneself.[1] Along with this feeling comes the fear of being *found out*, which can result in debilitating habits. In the context of writing academically, this can result in writer's block and intellectual paralysis. In community, this affects the degree to which an individual feels they are an integral part of a group. Beyond doctoral research and imposter syndrome, the notions of identity and belonging find their way into nearly every social interaction. Thus, SIT has both the benefit and risk of a very broad application. This chapter will unpack the elements of SIT which underpin this research into communal church identity.[2]

---

1. Bravata et al., "Commentary."

2. Some literature will refer to the metatheory of Social Identity, others will connect the various theories as spiritual successors to the original work of Tajfel and Turner. For our purposes, we will trace a specific line of theory which expands and at times corrects the original article.

SOCIAL IDENTITY THEORY

Henri Tajfel

Henri Tajfel was an individual who had a number of identities, some which became salient in certain situations. Often, deep aspects of a person's identity are formed through their home, their country, their faith, and their ethnicity. Initially named Heniek Tajfel, he was born in Poland into a Jewish home, staying there until he was seventeen.[3] He later reported discrimination which happened in Poland to the Jewish community during this time, and already during his youth he faced a dual identity of being of Polish nationality and maintaining Jewish traditions which were not always publicly acceptable.[4] Along with many other Jewish immigrants, he went to France in 1936 to study. While this may have seemed at first to be an improvement over the discrimination he faced in Poland, due to the large Jewish population in France, the situation in France was one which caused Tajfel to abandon many aspects of his Jewish identity for a season. This included his name, which was during this season permanently changed to Henri.[5] He intended to return home during the summer of 1939, but the failure of an exam resulted in him staying and retaking it, which caused him to avoid the invasion of Poland which likely would have cost him his life.[6] In November of 1939, Tajfel enlisted in the French army, and shortly after enlisting he became a prisoner of war through German capture. According to a colleague of Tajfel, during the war he was always at risk as a Polish Jew, and he lived under the false identity of a French Jew to preserve his life.[7]

After the war, Tajfel was left alone in Paris to deal with the death of his parents and over forty members of his family. He began working at a Jewish orphanage in Belgium called Villa Essor which was set up under Oeuvre de Secours aux Enfants, which was a non-government organization which aimed to provide practical assistance and care for Jewish people. Tajfel was popular among his students and intentionally removed elements of formality in order to reduce social distance from his students, including asking

---

3. Brown, *Henri Tajfel*, 13.

4. Brown, *Henri Tajfel*, 13.

5. Brown, *Henry Tajfel*, 20. It is not certain, but quite possible that this name change was to attempt assimilation. However, it is noteworthy that he did not change his surname which would have caused the same potential issues.

6. Brown, *Henry Tajfel*, 21.

7. Himmelweit, "Obituary," 288.

them to call him by his first name and using the informal *tu*.⁸ He switched homes, and at the second home began taking a number of courses. He was dismissed from his role at this new home due to a conflict with his supervisor and moved to Germany to work at a rehabilitation center providing support for disabled individuals and refugees.⁹ In 1951, he was laid off and applied to the University of London for a degree in psychology. His Polish secondary education and diploma which he took in Belgium were not accepted as prerequisites, so he took a qualifying exam and was accepted to begin a BA in Psychology beginning October 1951. A lecturer at the college noted (as an immigrant himself) that Henri was quite intellectual but also appeared to be an outsider, in particular due to his accent.[10]

Much more can be said about the life of Tajfel and can be explored in Brown, *Henri Tajfel*. However, the primary purpose of summarizing the early life of Henri Tajfel is to reveal how his life leading up to his academic career shaped his understanding and concerns of social identity, in-group relations, discrimination, and social belonging. Tajfel was at several times in his life forced to hide his national, cultural, and ethnic identity to preserve his life. Furthermore, during a time of transiency, he experienced firsthand the effects of discrimination and being an outsider. This leads us to his journal article and subsequent chapter entry, which is now quite well known, written along with his protégé John Turner. This article and chapter formed the basis for SIT, which is the theoretical framework within which this book is grounded.[11]

The Seminal Article and Experiments

In Tajfel and Turner "Social Identity," a framework was developed as a tool to explain intergroup conflict.[12] In this article, Tajfel described three components which intergroup membership has, namely the knowledge

---

8. Brown, *Henry Tajfel*, 59.
9. Brown, *Henry Tajfel*, 63, 65.
10. Brown, *Henry Tajfel*, 74.

11. In an overview of the life of Henri Tajfel, it is perhaps inappropriate to ignore the fact that he is reported to have engaged in sexual harassment and assault of many female students, including postgraduate students under his supervision. It is clear that he abused the power of his position, causing immense trauma for these individuals (Brown, *Henri Tajfel*, 153–59).

12. Tajfel, "Social Identity and Intergroup Behavior."

that an individual is a member of a group, an evaluative component (i.e., membership in a group may have positive or negative connotations), and an emotional component (i.e., emotions of individual and shared emotions of group).[13]

Tajfel unpacks the way in which an individual sees oneself as a part of a group and the way in which differentiation from other groups helps to form a positive social identity. He describes two extremes of social behavior which he calls interpersonal and intergroup behavior, admitting that the extreme ends of this spectrum are likely extremely rare.[14] With interpersonal behaviors, individuals act as individuals with group identity having no impact. Conversely, with intergroup behaviors, individuals act as members of a group with individual identity having no impact.

In 1970, Tajfel performed with colleagues a social experiment called the Minimal Group Experiments which became one of his most well-known works.[15] The goal of this experiment was to determine the minimal conditions in which participants would identify with a group rather than as individuals. The study divided the individuals into two groups and asked them to engage in resource allocation tasks. The participants chose resource allocation options that benefitted their own group, and also chose options which gave the greatest relative disadvantage for the other group even at the expense of their own group. There was a strategy of maximum difference as opposed to maximum in-group profit or maximum joint profit.[16] What was noteworthy about this experiment is the way in which the groups were formed. They were randomly selected, but they were falsely informed that the groupings had to do with their preference between the artists Paul Klee or Wassily Kandinsky. This experiment deconstructed explanations of group rivalry based solely on strong in-group identification. However, the minimal attribution of group identity is shown here to promote both in-group favoritism and intergroup discrimination. While this showed the unfortunate reality of our inherent need for opposition as human beings, this also revealed a deep sense of value in being within a group even through a minimal ascription. As Porter and Rosner summarize SIT, "We can understand membership in a social group as providing a source of individual

---

13. Tajfel, *Differentiation Between Social Groups*, 28–29.
14. Tajfel, "Social Identity and Intergroup Behaviour," 8–9.
15. Tajfel, "Experiments in Intergroup Discrimination."
16. Tajfel and Turner, *Social Identity Theory*, 14.

value and social organization. Simply put, I becomes We and Us, and You becomes They and Them."[17]

John Turner

SIT's seminal article was coauthored by Tajfel's protégé and colleague, John Turner. Unlike Tajfel, Turner did not face the severity of identity where life was threatened. However, he also entered this research with his own history surrounding identity, in-group belonging, and social dynamics. Turner was raised along with seven children in a small public housing apartment in London, UK. Turner was highly intelligent, earning a scholarship to the prestigious grammar school, Wilson's School. After completing his studies there, he enrolled in Sussex University.[18] However, according to an article published in the British Psychological Society, John Turner "never felt at home in the academic world."[19] He took six years to complete his degree due to multiple times dropping out of the program. During these times he would work, often taking employment alongside his father. At one point, he worked at a printing factory as a trades union organizer which became a formative experience in developing his own understanding of group identity. According to Haslam et al., this experience impressed on him the importance of groups in achieving social change. This also revealed to him the idea of power from individuals in subordinate positions coming from the combining force of group membership. This also made him aware of the dynamics of power dismantling and oppression, which underlie attacks on group rationality and decision.[20] This linkage of power struggles and group impact immensely shaped his later work on social identity.

Following the completion of his work at Sussex University, Turner began working on his PhD under the supervision of Henri Tajfel. This work began shortly after Tajfel had, alongside his colleagues, published the work of the minimal group experiment. Turner's PhD work helped to develop a theoretical framework to explain the findings of work which was developing on in-group conflict, relations, and group identity. The resulting dissertation attempted to demonstrate an inextricable linkage between social identity and social comparison. Turner argued that social competition

---

17. Porter and Rosner, "'All Things to All People,'" 290.
18. Haslam et al., "Identity, Influence, and Change," 202.
19. Haslam et al., "Identity, Influence, and Change," 202.
20. Haslam et al., "Identity, Influence, and Change," 203.

comes from the desire to resolve social comparisons in ways that favor an in-group.[21] This dissertation provided a starting point for future developments which would radically shape the field of social psychology. As a result of this interplay with Tajfel's work, following the conclusion of his PhD, Turner stayed at the University of Bristol to work with Tajfel on the task of developing a theoretical framework which came to be known as Social Identity Theory.[22]

Self-Categorizing Theory

The impact of John Turner on social psychology as it relates to SIT was far from over. In 1982, partially due to frustration with the British government and partially with a desire to expand on SIT, Turner spent a year as a visiting scholar at Princeton where he began to develop what came to be known as self-categorizing theory. This work continued during his time at Macquarie University in Sydney, Australia, where he worked with four PhD students to assist in the development of several key aspects of self-categorizing theory. Through this work, they developed the volume *Rediscovering the Social Group*. It is in this volume he, along with these students, showed the following:

1. attraction to individual group members is an outcome rather than simply a determinant of group identity;
2. the salience of self-categories is an interactive product of fit and accessibility;
3. group polarization is the product of group members' conformity to an extremitized group prototype;

---

21. Haslam et al., "Identity, Influence, and Change," 204.

22. It is important to note that the development of SIT does not end here. In chapter 3, I will explore one particular strand of development, whereby SIT has influenced organizational change through the development of the Identification with an Organizational Group Scale. For further work that has explored the relevance of SIT for leadership, see Hogg and Reid, "Social Identity, Leadership, and Power"; Hogg, et al., "Intergroup Leadership in Organizations"; Hogg, et al., "Social Identity Theory of Leadership"; Haslam et al., *New Psychology of Leadership*; Steffens, et al., "Social Identity Mapping"; Steffens, et al., "Leadership as Social Identity Management." Because my particular interest in SIT is not in directing leadership behavior but rather in self-reflection on the nature of identity, I am primarily interested in the foundational Tajfel/Turner developments rather than in the subsequent developments that have taken place in organizational and leadership studies.

4. crowd behavior reflects the situational elaboration of group norms and the power of members to act on them.[23]

Turner's work of Self-Categorization Theory expanded the work of SIT through focusing on the processes that take place within groups and between subgroups within a larger group rather than focusing on the processes that take place between groups.[24]

Turner expanded on social identity by looking at different levels of identity which have an impact on an individual. The first level involves the interaction of people as unique individuals. The second level is the group level, inclusive of subgroups and supergroups. The third level is where people interact based on the common identity of being human and common features shared by human beings.[25] However, Turner argued that group membership awareness is not enough to impact behavior; rather, the subjective *importance* of each group will determine one's actions in an actual situation.[26] The principle which Turner used to determine this subjective importance was the principle that a group will categorize themselves as a group to the degree that differences perceived between them are less than differences perceived between them and other people.[27] In other words, a group will find the grouping meaningful when they have more salient differentiation to outsiders than within those in their own community. The level of salience associated with a particular trait is not binary, and the various levels at which a group may find their group meaningful will shift significantly between various settings. For example, a small town may have residents who feel a deep sense of identity in their town due to the obvious differences between it and a nearby city. So, in contexts where there are both small town residents and city residents, the groupings based on location become salient. This has been shown, for example, in a recent study published in *Political Behavior* which shows that municipalities provide a meaningful social identity at levels similar to partisan identity for many individuals.[28] Through this study, Borwein and Lucas showed that a strong

---

23. Haslam et al., "Identity, Influence, and Change," 205.
24. Baker, "Social Identity Theory and Biblical Interpretation," 130.
25. Turner et al., *Rediscovering the Social Group*, 45.
26. Turner et al., *Rediscovering the Social Group*, 2.
27. Turner et al., *Rediscovering the Social Group*, 51–52.
28. Borwein and Lucas, "Municipal Identity and City Interests."

salience exists in Canadian cities as it pertains to municipal identity. Similarly, these subgroup identities can form within small groups to differentiate identity.[29]

Comparative Fit, Normative Fit, and Perceiver Readiness

According to John Turner, salience is a subjective category where a person's self-perception and behavior can change depending on what category is salient. Social categories emerge from stimuli that are organized into categories in such a way that within-category homogeneity and between-category heterogeneity are maximized. The metacontrast is the ratio of within- and between-category heterogeneity, which is calculated by dividing the average difference between categories by the average differences within a category.[30] The concept of salience clarifies the situational conditions under which group membership is perceived resulting in a behavioral influence. The salience of categorization, according to Turner, is a function of the interaction between how well the situation matches an existing or created category and the level at which the situation coheres with the person's understanding of that category.[31] Turner originally defined this interaction in terms of relative accessibility and fit. Fit exists in two categories: comparative and normative fit. Comparative fit refers to the relations between the persons compared, and normative fit refers to the agreement between stimulus persons compared and perceivers' preexisting stereotypical beliefs.[32] Relative

---

29. A significant recent development is the project Hafer et al., "Social Identity Dynamics." This project produced articles in three areas. First, the behavioral consequences of the links between social identity and the hyper-networked society, demonstrating that when people perceive inconsistency in others on social media, their interpersonal evaluations are influenced by the social identities they hold, as they use that information to judge the other's authenticity and motives on social media. The second area of investigation was how SIT can help explain in-group and out-group bias caused by individual decisions and behavior during the early stages of COVID-19, which led to collective outcomes for crowd behaviors. The final area investigated the role of identification with social identities in shaping individual differences in social media use, as well as how gender identification, traditional masculinity and femininity ideologies contribute to the goals of social media use during adolescence.

30. Turner et al., *Rediscovering the Social Group*.
31. Turner et al., *Rediscovering the Social Group*, 54–56.
32. Blanz and Aufderheide, "Social Categorization and Category Attribution."

accessibility involves what generally matches a specific setting as well as an individual's current motives.[33]

The category of relative accessibility has evolved in more recent literature to become the concept of perceiver readiness. Perceived readiness refers to how perception is constrained by the perceiver to reflect the perceiver's perspective at a given time.[34] Turner, et al. define this as "cognitive choice"—i.e., "the selective representation of phenomena from the vantage point of the perceiver."[35] In sum, comparative fit involves conceptual distances, where categorization is enhanced by creating categories with smaller distances *within* than *between*. Normative fit suggests that cognitive categories reflect features of category members and their categorization dimensions. Perceiver readiness depends on a perceiver's theories, expectations, knowledge, goals, motivations, and purposes. The level of saliency assigned to an identity will directly affect the level of impact which that identity has on the behaviors and experiences of individuals and groups. Therefore, within communities of faith, it is prudent to explore what salient identities exist which may be unknown and/or unspoken.

An important question may arise here: What about categories that are perceived by an individual to be important regardless of salience? For example, if an individual is of Scottish descent and feels a deep connection to the Scottish community—but this is not a salient part of their identity in their day-to-day interactions with others—where can this be described? This is where the categories of emphasis and trivialization are helpful. An individual will negotiate identities in interactive settings and this may result in an individual claiming an identity which others do not recognize.[36] In other words, identities are trivialized and emphasized in order of their personal importance for an individual, and this may not correspond to the salience of that identity, or even be an obvious identity to others.[37] A light-

---

33. Turner, "Social Comparison and Social Identity," 10–11.
34. McGarty, *Categorization in Social Psychology*, 115.
35. Turner et al., "Self and Collective," 462.
36. The work of Identity Theory (IT), a closely linked field from sociology, contains a very interesting link to this concept, particularly expressed in Brenner, "Causal Ordering." There has been work over time to integrate these theories, and while it is outside of the scope of research for this project, I am excited at the prospect of integrating the concepts of identity theory in future practical theological research.
37. IT uses a "multiple self" and identity prominence to describe variations in selves and identities (McCall and Simmons, *Identities and Interactions*). This has the same function as identity salience with the distinction that prominence reflects the ideal self of an

hearted example of this can be found in the character Ash from the 2009 film, *Fantastic Mr. Fox*. In this movie, Ash insists that he is an athlete and is convinced of this identity despite the lack of evidence in his abilities. He holds this identity dearly and emphasizes it despite those around him not identifying him as such and the identity not being apparent.[38] Within the communal context of a church or similar community, we can imagine a pastor with a perceiver readiness of a certain identity such as being a "youthful church" that neither the congregation nor the surrounding community would agree with. And, we can also imagine a similar situation where, over time, perceiver readiness will shift towards a certain identity.

Church leadership has a particular ability, primarily through perceiver readiness but also through affecting fit, to emphasize or trivialize certain beliefs, practices, or traits which are tied to both subgroup and group identities. An emphasis would represent the promotion of a particular trait as a determinant of communal identity, such as a focus on certain community practices or a particular theological doctrine. A trivialization would represent the demotion of a particular trait as a determinant of communal identity, such as a church leader who preaches to a politically polarized church the value of unity amidst diversity. This is shown visually with the below Trivial-Essential Spectrum (TES):

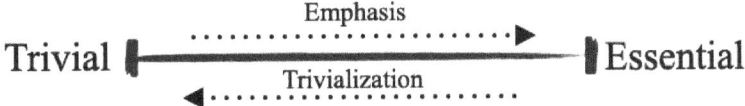

Figure 2: Trivial-Essential Spectrum

This spectrum demonstrates the manner in which normative fit can be adjusted by efforts to re-define what perceivers will regard as trivial and essential characteristics of group identity (i.e., perceiver readiness). The arrows reveal the potential that exists for self-aware church leaders to move particular group traits towards trivial or essential status. A trivialization will push a particular trait, such as a belief or practice or personal characteristic, away from the "official" definition of the community's "essential identity." It might be natural to assume that the goal should always to be to trivialize traits which differentiate in order to reduce barriers to belonging. However, emphasizing will often be important in connection with traits

---

individual.

38. Anderson, *Fantastic Mr. Fox*.

that are deemed particularly important to a church. This brings us back to the relationship between barriers to belonging and inherent exclusion. Belonging within a community of faith, as mentioned in the introduction, is defined in this book as the feeling or belief of being included within a community of faith, such that, as an individual, one functions as part of a wider church collective. Therefore, a high degree of belonging involves the perception of a shared identity. Yet the perception of group identities depends not only on perceived similarities and differences but also on the perceiver's readiness to identify a particular group in the first place, which depends in part on the individual's knowledge of normative fit (i.e., what stereotypical group members have in common).

Let us consider the individuals represented in figure 3:

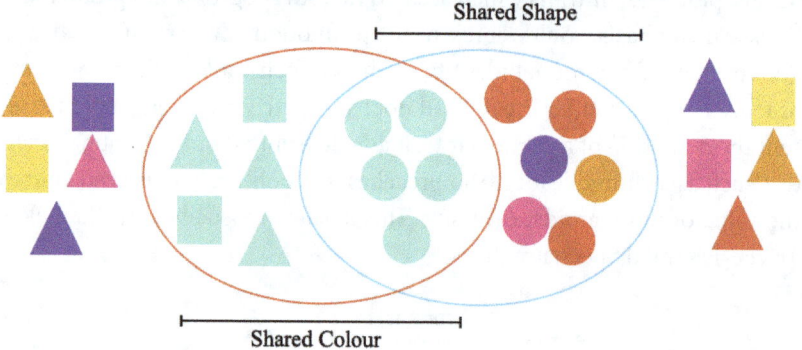

Figure 3: Visualization of Identities

In the above figure, we see two identities; namely, shape and color. The divisions represent those based on identity which are not related to the degree to which these divisions are enforced or minimized. We can imagine a grouping of the center green circles which has a clear in-group/out-group differentiation that arises from an essential (i.e., "official") group identity that includes being green and circle. This group identity presents a high barrier to belonging for individuals who are not green circles. These barriers could ultimately prevent those who do not share this identity from entering the community, unless the color represents a trait that is changeable.[39] To be clear, this does not necessarily mean the physical exclusion

---

39. Hannum (*Social Identity*) suggests three categories which can be used to map identity: given, chosen, and core. Given, chosen, and core identities form the basis of understanding personal and communal identity, with the interplay between these categories being crucial, especially within community contexts where defining "given" identity

Defining Congregational Identity

from gatherings—a "non-green circle" may even attend gatherings regularly and be permitted to do so—but they are less likely to experience deep belonging. By comparison, there may be another group in the same situation for whom "being green" is not an essential factor in communal identity. Here again, the green subgroup has a high likelihood of becoming salient, but the trivializing of their color as non-determinant for communal identity leaves open the possibility that individuals of other colors (but not necessarily other shapes) will feel a strong sense of belonging. For example, one might imagine that this group of circles defines itself over and against others that are mostly squares or triangles. Under such circumstances, even those circles that are marginal by virtue of their color may experience a profound sense of belonging—an experience that would be very much problematized by an "essential" green identity even amidst the same contrast with "out-group" squares and triangles. Indeed, because of the primacy of the circle identity, those who are yellow but not circles, in this example, find themselves differentiated regardless of the essential "green" identity. Notably, these dynamics can be both intentional and unintentional. For example, for one church, this may be having a Christian faith. While those without a Christian faith are welcome to attend and engage in the community, this church states that in order to enter fully into the community, a shared faith is required. Thus, the non-green circles represent those who do not share such an identity.[40] Another identity may be shared, represented by the trivial diagram, but is not a defining factor, or reason for exclusion. This shared identity exists nonetheless, but active measures are taken to reduce the barriers it causes.

As an example, one church I attended growing up ("Church A") had a worship style that many would call charismatic, with people raising their hands and moving around in worship.[41] Church A was experienced to be a

---

can be nebulous. Leaders navigating these categories must discern between established "given" identity and the potential for evolving the "core" identity through intentional choices. Clear communication and alignment within the community can mitigate barriers to belonging, fostering a cohesive sense of identity. In churches, denominational distinctions and governance structures contribute significantly to intentional identity formation, while unintentional identity factors may evolve over time, necessitating a nuanced approach to change.

40. In this visualization, there is neither meaning to proximity to the circle, nor proximity to the center. This is simply to demonstrate shared identities, and those who do not share that identity are "outside."

41. I am not referring here to any sort of theological stances, but rather the manner in which congregants physically respond to worship music.

charismatic church, in particular through a comparative fit of differentiation with other churches in the area. Yet I do not recall at Church A ever hearing guidance or encouragement towards worshipping in such a way, which allowed newcomers to decide for themselves whether or not they "fit in" enough to belong. By comparison, I once visited another church of the same affiliation ("Church B") and it displayed a more reserved style of worship. Church B had identical theological convictions to ours, officially, but would not have been perceived this way by uninformed newcomers. In both communities, therefore, it will have taken official messaging from the front in order for attendees to recognize that "charismatic" beliefs and practices were regarded as essential for members of the community (showing the importance of perceiver readiness and the role of leadership in influencing it). However, on yet another occasion, I was part of a group ("Church C") where the charismatic element was emphasized. Through clear teachings and a self-stated identity, we were guided to align with a particular worship style. All three of these churches had similar official identities, but leaders either emphasized or trivialized charismatic beliefs and practices, affecting the normative fit and perceiver readiness for people who came.

Church identities can also contain emphasized identities which are not particularly experienced. For example, all of the churches interviewed in this study place a high value on being culturally diverse, particularly in an increasingly culturally diverse country. However, these churches are also overwhelmingly white. Therefore, it is likely that the differentiation of ethnicity for people of color would be much more salient than it would be for the majority subgroup of white members. What is happening is that church leaders are trying to ensure that these potentially salient subgroup identities (i.e., ethnic groups) are not seen as determinant for normative fit. Whether this enables ethnic minorities to feel a sense of belonging will depend considerably on comparative fit (i.e., the extent to which ethnic differences within the church are outweighed by *other* differences between the church and alternative groups, in which case church membership may become quite salient and produce a real sense of belonging even for people who are visible minorities).

It is through this framework that we may find an avenue to navigate and develop useful data to unlock the "present" reality of church identity. The self-awareness of these aspects of identity can help to understand the perceiver readiness, comparative fit, and normative fit of the groupings with a congregation and how emphasis and trivialization affect this on the leadership level. The following list represents examples in the various categories as they may apply to churches:

- Trivialization: Within a congregation, there are polarized views on a particular issue. The pastoral team promotes focusing on other issues which they are united on and not allowing these issues to divide.
- Emphasis: A church is a part of a denomination with a particular theological position, and through sermons and classes, that position is promoted.
- Perceiver Readiness: Someone with a theological background who is aware of doctrinal differences may notice differences of thought that someone without this background finds less important.
- Comparative Fit: In a town with many different denominations represented, the differences between doctrine and worship style will be more salient. Further, one's experiences with different worship styles, leadership types, and the like will cause differences to be more noticeable.
- Normative Fit: A subgroup within a church believes that alignment with a certain belief is required to be biblically faithful. When the church shifts their position on that issue, the differentiation for that subgroup is much higher than for others.

Leaders must be aware of how comparative fit can highlight undesired identities, whether in relation to intergroup dynamics, such as a majority white church in an ethnically diverse neighborhood, or intragroup dynamics, such as unmarried members feeling excluded due to frequent focus on the value of marriage. Belonging arises from differentiation from outsiders, but it can be potentially disrupted by differentiation with other insiders. And all of this is impacted by normative fit, which involves the ways that individuals develop stereotyped understandings of group identity (i.e., what is our essential identity as a community, and hence what does a typical member look like?). For example, if a member of a church is one of only a few unmarried adults but has experienced a sense of acceptance and concluded that being single does not change their role within the church, this reflects a shift in perceiver readiness reducing the likelihood of a salient differentiation within the community making them feel out of place. Furthermore, church leaders face potential issues from any reduction in salience. Low salience at the congregational level may result in a lack of commitment from members, if the church fails to provide a distinctive identity. This can lead to internal conflicts, with intragroup (sub-)identities becoming those which are salient. Trivializing these (sub-)identities may reduce internal divisions through fostering a greater degree of in-group belonging, but only if the group comes to perceive its shared group identity as salient in relation to outsiders—which in turn may diminish newcomers' ability to imagine that they might experience a sense of belonging within the group.

SIT IN CHURCH LEADERSHIP

Churches often find themselves in a tension between idealized congregational identity, the subgroup and personal identities of their existing members, and the identities of those outside of the church. While the manner in which this manifests will differ between churches, the starting point for any church on determining communal identity and barriers to belonging is self awareness. As seen, this self-awareness is often driven in churches by the leadership team, and often the primary minister. In many churches' narratives, a specific drive such as a theological conviction helps the church navigate a difficult time and form a congregational identity. Over time, the normative fit of these identities will shift. Unless leaders are continually messaging the essential importance of the belief or practice, a gap can open up between the "official" identity and the actual group identity of the church. Jack Barentsen demonstrates this in his work proposing a social identity model of pastoral leadership. In this work, he examines how contemporary pastors and Paul in Corinthians grapple with adapting their churches' identities while also positioning themselves as prototypical community leaders. He shows that the process is frustrating and limited but also has tremendous potential. He also recommends further case studies that look not only explore pastoral leaders but the wider church and surrounding communities to gain insight for pastoral leadership.[42]

If these identities are actualized and addressed, there can be a strong differentiation between the identities of congregants due to the emphasis of a previously trivialized identity. As an example, suppose a pastor preaches a sermon on a doctrinal stance which is not usually preached on, and this alienates members who do not agree. Or, another example may be a church having a policy which is not consistently enacted. In these situations, the church leadership have to determine the importance of these various

---

42. Barentsen, "Church Leadership," 78–79.

practices and stances. Through the emphasis of these identities formed over a past theological distinction, the congregational identity of churches can develop into an internal differentiation, based on different understandings of group identity and hence different ways of evaluating normative fit through making those who disagree the enemy.[43] In other words, the comparative fit moves from highly differentiated to less differentiated. Church leaders may react through emphasis of a differentiated subgroup identity or through shifting the official congregational identity to align with the actual identity of the church.

Within communal studies of Christian churches, there will be many contextual factors which affect the salience of the subgroup and congregational identities of a church, both for in-group members and for out-group members. The strength of its salience will be determined by comparative fit, normative fit, and perceiver readiness. To the extent that a subgroup identity is made salient by comparative fit, each individual's sense of belonging will be impacted most significantly by how they perceive their own normative fit, which in turn is impacted by their perceiver readiness (i.e., their notion of what an ideal group member is like), which in turn is impacted (in part) by leadership actions with regard to defining what is "essential" to the community's identity (i.e., beliefs, practices, and traits that leaders think *should* be viewed as normative). Some examples of these areas which contribute to the aforementioned categories include theological agreements (divides), origins, tradition, shared statement, leadership structure, historical practices, and geographical location. In applying the concept of psychological salience to the leadership tasks of emphasis and trivialization, we can think in terms of forces that can either strengthen or weaken an individual's perception of a communal identity and of their (non-)belonging to a particular church community. We can imagine this tension as two teams in a tug of war match.

---

43. Fitch, *Church of Us vs. Them*, 36.

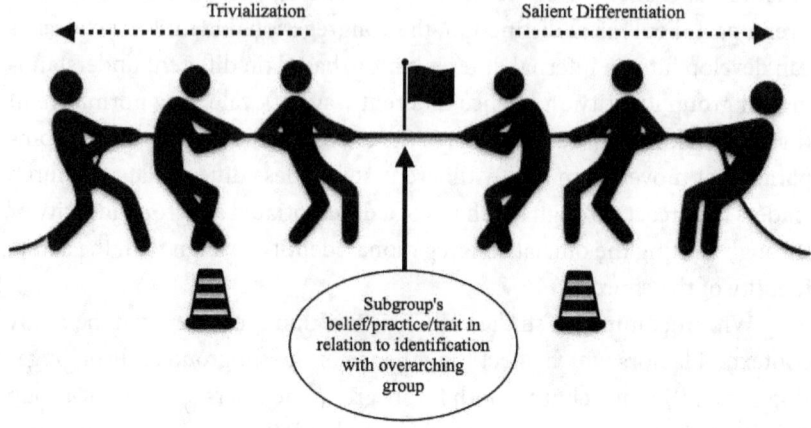

Figure 4: Tug of War

This should not be misunderstood to indicate that salient and trivialized identities are always at odds, but rather to demonstrate the psychological and leadership forces which are often at play towards differentiated subgroup identities. These differentiated subgroup identities can include any belief, practice, or trait that might give rise to a perceived group identity. These will sometimes be exclusive to a specific group through defining against an out-group, but are also shared within a metagroup. The identities explored in churches will include intergroup identities (the identity of being part of the group of the church vs. other identities) and intragroup identities (the various identity groupings which exist within a church community). The salient differentiation of these identities are in an ongoing tension with trivialization of such differentiation, and church leaders will often need to decide how much "force" is appropriate to apply to trivializing these differences.

INTERPLAY OF SUBGROUP IDENTITIES

I have defined belonging as the feeling or belief of being included within a group, with the belief that as an individual, one also functions as part of a wider collective. Therefore, barriers to belonging are factors (whether beliefs, practices, or other traits) which hinder the feeling of being included within a community of faith, with the belief that as an individual, one also functions as part of the wider collective. Crucially, "barriers" of this sort can occur either among members or among non-members. Among members of a group, reduced belonging can be the result of feeling marginal, in the sense of not aligning with what is seen to be typical of group members (i.e., low normative fit). It can also be the result of emerging intragroup divisions, which reduce the salience of the overall group identity and attract feelings of belonging towards subgroups (i.e., high subgroup salience and low group salience). Among non-members of a group, reduced belonging is the result of actually *being* marginal, in the sense of not aligning with group identity at all but rather aligning with a salient alternative. Yet even still, we can explore degrees of non-belonging. Perhaps perceived differences are just matters of misperception and they can be cleared away with careful conversation (i.e., reduced perceptions of low normative fit). Also, insofar as there will be many overlapping beliefs, practices, and traits shared by both in-group and out-group members, these overarching commonalities can be brought into focus and this can reduce feelings of non-belonging and make it more likely that an outsider feels comfortable (i.e., high meta-group salience and low group salience).

This idea of barriers to belonging can be imagined by figure 5, which represents how strongly in-group members feel that they belong to a group.

Low barriers
of belonging

High barriers
of belonging

Figure 5: Barrier Circle Diagram

When we place someone in this diagram towards the center of the circles, for that individual there are low barriers to belonging with respect to a particular belief, practice, or trait. Low barriers here does not only mean that there are fewer unnecessary steps to enter, but also reflects a lower degree of differentiation between respective individuals experiencing the belief, practice, or trait.[44] Given the aforementioned categories, we can imagine

---

44. These principles are also true in the formation of churches. For example, if a white, middle-class, rural Canadian forms a church around their own identity, there may be significant barriers to belonging for those outside of that identity which are not

that barriers to belonging emerge from differentiation through perceiver readiness, comparative fit, and normative fit. As a person moves away center of the circle, barriers to belonging increase.

To demonstrate this principle, I will use a situation which is a common source of conflict within Canadian churches, namely, the blending of different styles of musical worship, commonly called "worship wars."[45] This situation will be demonstrated using the aforementioned diagram. When only a traditional style of worship is used, the red group experiences a very low barrier to belonging. When only a modern style of worship is used, the reverse is true.

Figure 6: Worship Wars—Divided Identity

Suppose this church, as an experiment, brings a blended style of worship in the congregation for a period of six months. At the end of the six months, the same individuals are surveyed to determine their levels of belonging during musical worship, resulting in the "Blended Worship" figure. Perhaps the lead pastor may be disappointed at first when she gets these results, hoping that the blended worship style would lower barriers and hence create belonging for everyone. She may have been hoping to see most people directly in the center, feeling a very strong sense of belonging. Instead, there is a net movement towards the center, but with fewer individuals directly in the center. The goal of this example is not to make a comment on

---

easily seen by fellow white, middle-class, rural Canadians. In this example, the distinctive identities are obvious, but often background, personal stories, and other unseen factors will complexify this.

45. The issue of "worship wars" has also been explored in a number of works such as Byars, *Future of Protestant Worship*; Herl, *Worship Wars*; Van Dyken, "Worship Wars"; Ruth, "Eruption of Worship Wars." Within SIT, Johnson, "Worship Styles" is an interesting study which used SIT to examine the conflict which occurs in churches over music style during worship services. This study found that a stronger identification with the Lutheran larger organization related to a preference for traditional or formal worship components. Also, a DPT collogue of mine has recently written a dissertation on congregational singing shaping social identity within Cantonese worship services (Mok, "Congregational Singing").

the role of traditional versus modern music in Christian worship, nor to suggest any sort of solution to this issue. Rather, the purpose is to view a particular practice within a context through the lens of SIT. With respect to a particular belief, practice, or trait, it may be that a certain course of action will contribute towards a deeper sense of belonging for some individuals but set up barriers to belonging for others. A church may be able to determine a course of action which they believe is best given the available data, but these actions need to be based on self-awareness of the actual nature of the practices within a church rather than assumptions or self-definition. Leaders need to be mindful of the ways that people are likely to experience belonging (or lack thereof) in relation to particular beliefs, practices, or traits.

Self-awareness is also important because practices may cause barriers to belonging that are contrary to the community's stated purposes. As a result, defining the "why" for activities that affect the community's identity can be challenging. For example, one group of members may believe that their church's primary mission is to reach out to nonbelievers, while another believes that their mission is to empower community members, and yet another believes that they are called to address social injustices in their surrounding communities. Because of this complexity, an ideal or acceptable "balance of belonging" may be different not only for different churches but for different congregational members, and it may not be possible in practice to enable everyone to feel that they belong.

It is worth noting that belonging arises from many different factors, and that group members can often accept a scale of belonging for a given belief, practice, or trait even when they do not view themselves as close to the resulting center. Thus, a congregant's "ideal" scale can be described as the scale they believe would be optimal for representing their community's idealized identity, regardless of where they themselves fall along the scale. In the above example, a congregant may experience a stronger feeling of belonging when just traditional music is performed, but believe that a mutual compromise is required to deepen the collective community, and thus find the third scale to be the best fit for the community. They might even accept their own marginalization, if they deem that the playing of only more progressive music will better align with the community's ideal congregational identity. This helps to reveal that, although the focal point of this study is on leader self-awareness, the congregation itself has a role in the potential emphasis or trivialization of a particular belief, practice, or trait.

TEST SCALE

With the focal point of this study being an exploration of the effectiveness of this framework in assisting church leader self-awareness, there exists the reality of the complex nature of the theoretical material discussed thus far. This became obvious during the presentation phase of my research as I attempted to lay out with the pastoral leaders the framework which lay under the qualitative data. As such, one of the outcomes of this study is a visual aid to demonstrate the complex interworkings of these principles within churches. This scale is referred to as the Trivial-Essential-Salience Transformation (TEST) Scale.

This scale is not an attempt to describe all that occurs within communal identity, nor a model that will describe every possible factor in church identity. Instead, the TEST Scale has been created with the practice of self-aware Christian leadership in mind. This is a qualitative tool which helps to visualize comparative snapshots of subgroup differentiation both to clarify synchronic differences involving different subgroup identities and to envisage diachronic differences arising from real or projected changes over time. This serves as a descriptive framework for analysis and understanding.

In order to explain the TEST scale, I will discuss each of the individual components which make it up. To begin, the scale has a dot (or multiple dots). The dot(s) on a TEST scale represents the impact of a belief, practice, or trait of a subgroup within a group, with a greater green shaded area indicating greater impact. Within this study, the "group" always represents a particular church community.[46] Thus, the dot represents the impact of a belief, practice, or trait of a subgroup identity on belonging in the congregation. For example, the impact of age of millennials on belonging in Church X (trait), the impact of small group ministry participation of new members on belonging in Church X (practice), or the impact of espousing a particular belief concerning biblical inerrancy on belonging in Church X (belief). In addition, there may be times where the scale can be used to describe an intragroup identity which is also a subgroup within the wider community, such as second generation immigrants within the immigrant

---

46. The TEST scale explores the impact of a belief, practice, or trait of *subgroup x* on belonging within *group y*. In order to best address the primary goal of church leadership self-awareness of congregational identity, within this study *group y* is always a particular church. However, there remain other potential uses where *subgroup x* is the actual congregation, and *group y* is a wider community such as the surrounding neighborhood, the wider denomination, etc.

community at Church X. Importantly, the dot does not highlight the actual practice, belief, or trait, but the impact of the practice, belief, or trait on a subgroup as regards their belonging in a particular church.

The Y axis of the TEST scale represents the degree to which a salient differentiation occurs for the particular subgroup relative to a particular belief, practice, or trait. The degree to which a dot will rise or fall on the Y axis will be determined by salience of a subgroup identity in a particular congregational setting. The way that people respond to heightened salience will depend considerably on their perceptions of group and subgroup identity, especially as regards the trait, belief, or practice of the identity that has become salient. This would exist most clearly in the cases where membership of a group is clearly restricted. This occurred for me as a pastor when I was invited to join the monthly seniors' lunch that was taking place at the church. At first, I felt like my identity as a young adult in a group that was otherwise restricted to elderly people was very salient. However, over time, the impact of my age was trivialized as a factor in belonging to this group.

An extremely low salience on this scale would represent a situation where a particular part of a person's identity bears little to no impact, positively or negatively, on their sense of belonging. Further, this identity would not be noticeable, relevant, or interesting to others. While low salience can occur in a situation where there is little diversity between a belief, practice, or trait of a subgroup and the wider group (such as being male at a boys-only school), salience can increase in a low-diversity situation if attention is drawn to it (such as the school having a talk on the differences between male and female). Furthermore, low salience can occur in situations where there is a clearly visible difference but no attention is drawn to it (such as being the only glasses-wearer at a party).

Conversely, extremely high salience occurs when a particular aspect is one of the most clear aspects of a subgroup within a particular group, and it would be virtually impossible to not notice. A humorous example of this occurred for myself and my wife when we attended a Saskatchewan Roughriders CFL Grey Cup party wearing the gear of our favorite team, the Hamilton Tiger-Cats. In that moment, our trait as "Ti-Cat" fans within the wider group of that party was, given the context and the converse identities, extremely salient.

The X axis of the TEST scale helps to clarify an important way that church leaders can influence belonging in the midst of salient differentiation.[47] The X axis is, in essence, the aforementioned Trivial-Essential Spectrum, with the added middle point of "neutral." The X axis represents the impact of actual or possible interventions on the part of churches and their leaders with respect to the relevant trait, belief, or practice as a component of congregational identity. Emphasizing involves attempts to move the dot towards essential—that is, intentionally promoting the belief, or practice, or trait as integral to group identity. Trivialization involves attempts to move the dot towards trivial, thereby minimizing the belief, practice, or trait as non-essential to group identity. For example, the seniors' group which invited me to their lunch made an effort to trivialize age as non-essential for group participation. Notice that here again the scale does not prescribe anything, and it will have different implications depending on the identities in view. This group could have chosen to not invite me, as doing so would reduce the ability for the group to have a time set-aside to gather with peers. However, this group emphasized the common relationship I had with the members of the group as the pastor and (as far as I was aware) felt that no one's experience would be hindered by my presence. This example is a very obvious contrast of identities—namely, age related. However, within churches, these can be much more subtle, and it can be complex to assess what trivialization or emphasis will do to the group and subgroup identities. For example, if a theological belief gets emphasized as essential to community identity, this will have implications for individuals who espouse the belief, as well as for people who do not, and the result could be that certain people feel they do not at all belong. A dot which would be extremely trivial would be a belief, practice, or trait which no one feels is important to group identity. A dot which would be extremely essential would be a belief, practice, or trait which one must have in order to be a part of the group.

We then combine the X and Y axes, drawing connecting lines to help to show a striking visual image that captures the extent to which experiences of (non-)belonging are likely to arise for individuals in the relevant subgroup due to the relative salience of their identity as a subgroup as well as their perceptions of how essential the subgroup's trait, belief, or practice is to the overarching congregation's identity.[48]

47. Church leaders are not the only people who can emphasize or trivialize, and indeed typically a congregational "buy-in" would be needed in order to do so successfully.

48. As a point of clarification, no part of the TEST scale represents a mathematical plot and the common attributes of a linear graph do not apply. It provides no quantitative data on either salient differentiation or emphasis/trivialization. Instead, the TEST

A scale can refer to the impact of belonging or non-belonging of the respective subgroup within the overarching group identity. Whether a chart indicates belonging or non-belonging is determined by whether the "dot" matches or diverges from the stereotypical prototype of the overarching group. That stereotype can be determined by several factors which may or may not be determined by church leadership (e.g., a church which naturally has people gathering for coffee as opposed to a church where the value of after-church fellowship has been promoted).

Cape Town Example

To demonstrate a use of this scale, I will draw on a 2019 South African study which focused on the insider-outsider divide found between refugees and citizens. Drawing upon both the study and other research, Dickie reports,

> Although a number of churches in Cape Town include refugees among their regular attendees, few citizens make a concerted effort to reach out to these marginalised people (or indeed any on the fringes), as they are often caught up in their own lives and blind to the needs and burdens of others. . . . Negative stereotypical views about refugees are fairly widespread. . . . Despite their best attempts to fit in, many foreigners still find themselves ostracised, with the associated deep pain it causes.[49]

Therefore, the Cape Town refugee subgroup finds a very salient differentiation not only relative to the wider community but also within the church itself, and so the dot representing this subgroup should be plotted within the high range along the Y axis. The placement of the dot along the X axis will be determined by each church's approach to the differentiation felt by a refugee congregant. If a congregation were to actively perpetuate negative stereotypes of refugees and thereby to cast refugees as an out-group, we would need to plot immigration status as an emphasized factor in group membership (red dot). Far more likely, however, is a community that

---

scale is a visual tool to help leaders contemplate alternative experiences, whether real or hypothetical. Although in principle we should plot each different subgroup with its own dot, in certain cases we can use a single dot for multiple subgroup identities because they are defined inversely as either including or excluding some trait, belief, or practice and so they will produce salience or become subject to leadership efforts in identical ways but with inverse implications (i.e., salience and/or leadership efforts will affect two opposite groups, resulting in greater belonging for one and greater non-belonging for the other).

49. Dickie, "Building Community," 51.

unthinkingly caters its programming to non-refugees (for instance, by engaging in practices that present barriers to refugees). This scenario would involve neither emphasis nor trivialization (yellow dot). Alternatively, a congregation might intentionally strive to welcome refugees with words and practices that enable the perception of refugees as potential group members, in which case the dot would be plotted as trivializing immigration status as not a significant criterion for group membership (green dot). We then draw lines to show the shapes that results from the dot(s). This provides a visualization of the extent to which being a refugee affects the degree of belonging which is likely to occur.

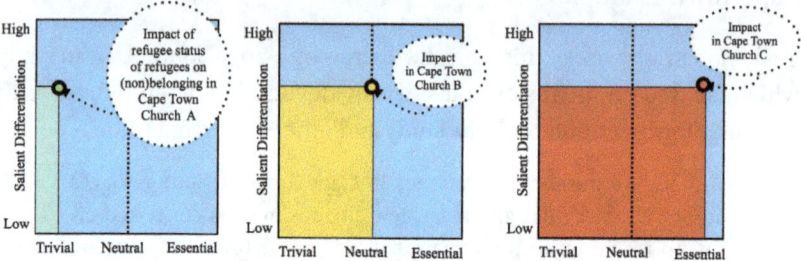

Figure 7: TEST: Refugees in Cape Town Churches

In the right graph (Church C), there is a high level of non-belonging for refugees. This is not unexpected—it is intuitive that pushing against an already marginalized group will further make that group feel like outsiders. More importantly, a church that does nothing will still cause visiting refugees to experience some non-belonging due to the inevitable salience of being a refugee surrounded by non-refugees (yellow graph). The green graph, in contrast, represents a church making an effort to reduce the degree to which a person's refugee status affects their sense of belonging in a congregation.[50]

The unnamed church which was studied by Dickie appears to have been similar to the "yellow dot" in relation to the subgroup of refugees.[51]

[50]. It is worth repeating for clarification that belonging for the purposes of this project is non-binary and fluid. For example, a relatively higher degree of belonging should not be thought to mean that in common language "they belonged"; rather it is within the aforementioned context of the SIT categories of in-group/out-group identity.

[51]. While the study of the unnamed local church does not provide extensive data of the church prior to the experiment, the reports of refugees seem to confirm that their experience within the church would fall within the neutral category (i.e., experiencing salience due to being different, but not actively excluded). However, it is difficult to make a definite conclusion with what was taught or spoken regarding refugees prior.

Dickie then invited a group of refugees to participate in a study which would compose personal laments from which a communal lament was formed, framed by scriptures which highlighted Christian unity. The congregation was invited to the front to surround the refugees as a symbol of "insiders" protecting and blessing "outsiders." The hope of this was that "by exposing church members to some of the difficulties experienced by fellow Christians who happen to be refugees, their attitude would change, and they would become more empathic."[52] Congregants were asked to complete a questionnaire assessing previous contact with refugees and gauging whether their attitude toward refugees had changed. Overwhelmingly, the respondents had stated that they became more aware of issues faced by refugees and the problems which were faced.[53] The church congregation had a shift in perceiver readiness towards the refugee population. The refugees who participated in the study experienced it as a symbolic opening of the churches arms to them.[54]

Returning to the TEST scale, this event would likely not decrease but instead increase the already high salience of the refugee subgroup differentiation, because even more attention was drawn to their atypical status within the wider community. However, this will have been combined with a strong movement towards the trivialization of this differential, resulting in a slight reduction in the impact of their refugee status on their experience of non-belonging.[55] The below graphic shows the case study of the Cape Town church with the visualization of the TEST Scale. While salience does increase, the overall impact of refugee status on non-belonging decreases. As the church was unnamed in the study, it is referred below simply as "Cape Town Church."

Regardless, it is clear that there was a general movement from a more neutral approach to a trivialization of differentiation due to immigration status as a result of the actions of the church leadership.

52. Dickie, "Building Community," 57.
53. Dickie, "Building Community," 59.
54. Dickie, "Building Community," 60.
55. This example gives a helpful opportunity to further clarify that trivialization, despite what may be implied by the name, does not mean pretending that something does not exist or that it is bad. To the contrary, trivialization represents efforts such as to reduce the differentiation experienced by particular subgroups by reframing the overarching group identity in a way that minimizes the importance of the subgroup differentiation.

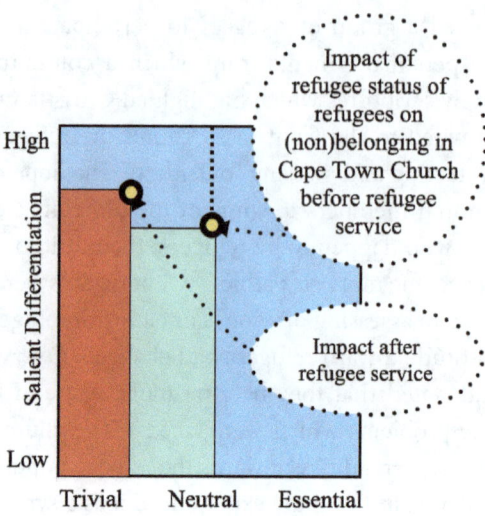

Figure 8: TEST: Refugees in Cape Town Church

We do not have subsequent data of the church following this experiment, but it is possible that over time, as this trivialization became engrained in the normative fit of the refugee subgroup, the salience of their identity as refugees will have decreased from the passing of time, shared experiences with the wider churches, outside factors, and other potential forces. It is also not possible for all practices or identities to always foster deep belonging and be widely inclusive. A church's values will determine which identities that are part of their collective identity represent "who we want to be," and which identities represent "who we don't want to be." Churches are also influenced by "what happens," which refers to people's reactions and perceptions. This could be due to a variety of reasons, both internal and external.

American Political-Religious Affiliation Example

My second example of the TEST Scale will explore a cultural trend in religious affiliation in relation to right-wing politics, from Hout and Fischer, "Why More Americans Have No Religious Preference."[56] This study

56. This particular study provides a helpful extensive overview of a subgroup finding increasing non-belonging with a religious group, for the purpose of demonstrating the TEST Scale. However, it should be noted that there is much that can be engaged on this topic in interacting with recent events—in particular following COVID-19 and

explores the reasons for declining religious affiliation among the growing religious "nones." It showed that in contrast with a commonly held belief that the rise of nones is tied to religious skepticism, those who identified as non-religious held conventional religious beliefs. While there was some growth that was tied to the succession of non-religious practices (i.e., the children of non-religious people tended to be non-religious), the majority of the increase of non-religious identity was from "unchurched believers"—that is, those who identify as non-religious but hold religious beliefs. A key finding of this study is that the increase in non-religious identity was tied to political moderates and liberals; the religious preferences of political conservatives did not change.[57] While this particular study did not explore whether this was due to political/religious events such as the rise of the "religious right" (as this was outside the scope of this study), it found a connection between individuals' view of political activism within churches and the rise of religious nones. Over seven years (1991–1998), there was a polarization in views around whether church leaders should attempt to influence congregants' votes and governments' decisions. Those who held positions of "strongly agree" or "strongly disagree" increased while those holding a view of agree, neutral, or disagree decreased.[58]

While this study was not focused on a particular church, we can plot an "average American church" (referred henceforth as AAC) where these trends were occurring. The below right scale represents the politically moderate subgroup attending this church in 1990.[59]

American presidential events. As such, the topic of the intersection of political and religious identity is very extensive and ongoing. Some examples of these studies include Packard and Ferguson, "Being Done"; Campbell, "Acts of Faith"; Reed, "Emerging Treason?" and Hemler, "American Faith Adrift."

57. Hout and Fischer, "Why More Americans," 165.
58. Hout and Fischer, "Why More Americans," 187.
59. I use political moderates as an example, but the same would likely be true of political liberals.

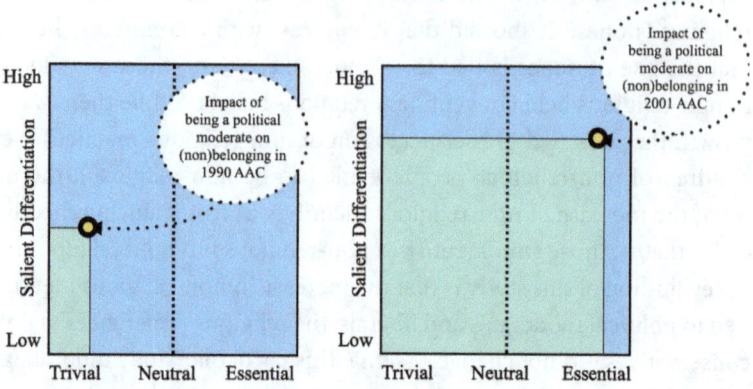

Figure 9: TEST: Political Moderates in 1990 vs 2001 AAC

This group may find themselves existing in an environment where the leaders of the church hold opposing political views, but the salient differentiation between this subgroup and the wider congregation is not significant. It may rise and fall—for example, during elections—but it does not reach a level where it significantly alters belonging. However, ten years later, we see a rise in salient differentiation. Those who are politically moderate find their subgroup identity significantly more salient within the Average American Church.[60] The right scale in figure 9 represents the same group with a growth in salient differentiation, assuming a growing emphasis on conservative politics as essential to communal identity (e.g., conservative political sermons, events, involvement) in 2001.

A church that wants political moderates to feel welcomed despite the fact that they may be in the minority will need to see the dot move towards trivial. Perhaps a conservative church promotes the idea that although there is a general trend among them towards political conservatism, this is an unimportant aspect of being the church. This would have the effect on political moderates of reducing the impact of being a political moderate as a factor in (non)belonging to the church. Thus, the TEST scale acts as a snapshot of current and potential realities, and it can be used by leaders in order to explore the identity of a congregation.

---

60. This assumption is rooted in the aforementioned finding that political moderates/liberals who identified as religious nones made up the majority of the increase of non-religious identification. Of course, there were within this period churches which highlight political neutrality and liberal ideology, but these reflect the average within the growing religious "nones" who were explored in this study.

Conclusion

As demonstrated through this exploration, Social Identity Theory is profoundly relevant to the church. The theory's role in understanding intergroup dynamics and its application in deciphering the complexities of social identity, belonging, and behavior provide invaluable insights for church leaders. Jack Barentsen provides a useful summary of the applicability of SIT to practical theology,

> Moreover, identity is not only a theological category ('the people of God') or a spiritual reality ('my identity in Christ') but is embedded in religious and social discourse and group dynamics. Faith communities have vital exclusive faith claims while often engaging their civic community more inclusively—all matters of socio-religious identity. Pastoral care benefits from paying attention to the dynamics of socio-religious identification as a factor in spiritual wellbeing. In short, social identity theory enlightens the psychological and social dimensions of the relational nature of being human.[61]

SIT helps to complexify and describe the nature of communal identity. In utilizing SIT, church leaders can grow in their understanding of how social identities shape the dynamics within their congregation. The remaining chapters will explore a narrative inquiry into utilizing the tools of SIT to foster leadership self-awareness in congregational identity.

---

61. Barentsen, "Understanding Peace and Conflict," 322.

CHAPTER 3

Research Scope

COMMUNITIES OF FAITH STRUGGLE greatly with recognizing their own shared communal identity. This can result in difficulties communicating their values to others, inconsistency between their perceived and actual communal identities, and difficulty adapting to changes within their community or society as a whole. However, by actively engaging in self-reflection and dialogue with community members, faith communities can better comprehend and articulate their congregational identity and the subgroup identities that exist within and around it, resulting in a stronger sense of unity and purpose. By utilizing the tools of Social Identity Theory and narrative inquiry, faith communities can gain a deeper understanding of their community, resulting in a community that is more cohesive and purposeful.

NARRATIVE INQUIRY

The present study is a qualitative research project that undertakes a narrative inquiry. Through the analysis of personal narratives, the study aims to gain a deeper understanding of the experiences and perspectives of individuals with the intention of exploring how qualitative methods can foster self-awareness among church leaders. Qualitative research methods are frequently used to investigate complex and subjective topics, and narrative research is especially effective at revealing the nuances and interpretations engrained in personal stories.[1] Through this research, a more comprehensive understanding of church-based communal identity will be developed.

Background of Narrative Inquiry

Narrative inquiry is a research method that focuses on the stories or narratives that individuals share about their experiences.[2] It evolved from the study of literature. This approach is commonly utilized in the social sciences and can yield valuable insights into the lived experiences of individuals and communities. Through narrative analysis, researchers can identify themes and patterns that can inform policy and practice.

It is difficult to pinpoint a seminal origin point for narrative inquiry. In certain aspects, narrative inquiry has existed throughout human history. Late in the twentieth century, however, there were numerous developments aimed at clarifying and defining narrative inquiry, which were then adopted as a data interpretation model for human subjects as a number of influential publications have helped define and clarify certain aspects of narrative inquiry as a research methodology. The book *Narrative Knowing and the Human Sciences* serves as a bridge between narrative research in literary criticism and the social sciences. In addition, Polkinghorne makes references to works of history and philosophy, relating the methodologies employed by these disciplines to a method in human science.[3] Another key development is found in the publication of the *Handbook of Narrative Inquiry*, which describes four historical turns that direct the flow of inquiry into a narrative channel. These include a shift in the relationship between researcher and researched, a shift from using numbers to words as data, a shift from a focus on the general and universal to the local and particular, an acceptance of a broader range of ways of knowing, and a blurring of epistemologies in research.[4] Social identities include individual and group views, and these groups "will create shared 'life stories' or narratives of the group which tie past, present and predicted futures into a coherent representations."[5]

1. Busetto et al., "Use and Assess."
2. Karpa, "Narrative Inquiry Methodology."
3. Polkinghorne, *Narrative Knowing*.
4. Clandinin, *Handbook of Narrative Inquiry*.
5. Cinnirella, "Exploring Temporal Aspects," 235.

Narrative Inquiry in Studies of Congregations

Narrative inquiry is used in congregational studies to investigate the stories of church members and leaders. The undermentioned examples demonstrate the value of narrative inquiry in probing the complex and nuanced aspects of human experience and behavior. By analyzing the narratives of church members and leaders, researchers gain insight into the personal beliefs, motivations, and struggles that shape their experiences as a congregation. This qualitative approach allows for a deeper understanding of how individuals navigate their faith and engage with others in a religious setting. While research projects may not explicitly state that they use narrative methodology, they do often rely heavily on narrative inquiry to extract meaningful data from congregational studies.

A significant work related to my own project is the Boston University research project, "Spiritual Narratives in Everyday Life," undertaken by principle investigator Nancy Ammerman.[6] This project sought to explore the ways in which spiritual frameworks and sensibilities influence everyday life and relationships. Stories were analyzed from ninety-five participants in Boston and Atlanta in order to identify patterns of presence and absence in religious settings. The study involved interviews, photographs, and digital recorders to explore the impact of religious and spiritual elements on daily life. The findings aimed to explore how these elements influence work and family life and provide a starting point for understanding modern religious lives. Out of this work, a number of helpful publications emerged. Ammerman maps religiousness among a significant portion of contemporary American religion, suggests a research agenda for the future, and demonstrates the potential of lived religion for shaping theories that can better map the relationship between religiousness and religion.[7] Ammerman also analyzes this data to show that the distinction between spirituality and organized religion fails to capture the empirical reality of American religion and the complexity of spirituality.[8] Williams explores the ways people make space for God in everyday settings, focusing on the dimensions, power, and meaning of sacred spaces, which often extend their power beyond institutional boundaries.[9]

---

6. Ammerman, "Spiritual Narratives in Everyday Life."
7. Ammerman, *Sacred Stories, Spiritual Tribes*.
8. Ammerman, "Spiritual but Not Religious?"
9. Williams, "Space for God."

Ganzevoort, "Narrative Approaches" provides a brief overview of the narrative method of inquiry and its use in practical theology. He highlights non-exhaustively three avenues taken by narrative approaches. These include narrative forms in faith communication such as preaching, empirical analysis and deconstruction of religious subjectivity, and the empowerment of marginalized voices by creating an audience for them which previously did not exist.[10] Narrative structure influences the study of how our lives exist narratively and how meaningful action and interpretation can be interpreted.[11] With this assumption, hermeneutical theories and methods are applied to social sciences and practices, interpreting not only traditional textual and narrative elements but also rituals, exchanges, and actions. In order to include these various non-textual faith elements within the narrative approach, a helpful definition of narrative would be that it "includes all forms of representation of real or fictional situations in a time sequence. This sequence connects events into patterns of causality, desirability, development, and meaning."[12]

Stephen Crites, in his seminal piece on narrative research in theology, writes of the embodied action nature of the narrative experiences, explaining,

> If experience has the narrative quality attributed to it here, not only our self-identity but the empirical and moral cosmos in which we are conscious of living is implicit in our multidimensional story. It therefore becomes evident that a conversion or a social revolution that actually transforms consciousness requires a traumatic change in a man's story. The stories within which he has awakened to consciousness must be undermined, and in the identification of his personal story through a new story both the drama of his experience and his style of action must be reoriented.[13]

In this article, Crites points to a sort of musical, dramatic story which is told together by a congregation. The narratives which exist within a congregation sometimes are simply the communal side of such stories, namely the discipleship and evangelism within a church body and care which is reflected as such. Deeper stories within congregations may reveal immovable

---

10. Ganzevoort, "Narrative Approaches," 214.
11. Ganzevoort, "Narrative Approaches," 215.
12. Ganzevoort, "Narrative Approaches," 216.
13. Crites, *Narrative Quality of Experience*, 307.

principles, hidden assumptions, or power struggles which would not have been at first obvious.

James Hopewell writes of three functions of narratives within congregational life: the congregation's self-perception is primarily narrative in form, the congregational communication is primarily narrative, and by congregating, the congregation participates in the narrative structures of society.[14] Ganzevoort, "Narrative Approaches" offers a configuration which encapsulates many of these facets through a six-dimensional approach. The selection and connection of the elements through structure is used through a time sequence given in a particular order. The author frames the narrative within a certain perception which is interpreted in light of gender, age, ethnicity, and other power structures at play. The charge of the story is defined by its tone in the ability of the narrative to reach the aims of the author. The roles which are assigned to the various characters of the story imparts an important dimension which offers an essential element of the process. Relational propositioning is the process by which the narrator uses the story with an audience and the intended accomplishments in the telling of the story. Similarly, justification for an audience is judged by the criteria the audience holds and the constellation of the audience.[15]

The narrative aspect of communities is a primary source for formation of marginal Christian communities. Christians do not primarily form an argumentative reasoning community but rather a storytelling community.[16] In *Mighty Stories, Dangerous Rituals*, Anderson and Foley speak to the human experience as interconnected with fundamental elements of the narrative approach:

> Human experience is structured in time and narrative. We comprehend our lives not as disconnected actions or isolated events but in terms of a narrative. We conceive of our lives as a web of stories—a historical novel or a miniseries in the making. We think in stories in order to weave together into a coherent whole the unending succession of people, dates, and facts that fill our lives. The narrative mode, more than other forms of self-reporting, serves to foster the sense of movement and process in individual and communal life. In that sense, the narrative framework is a human

---

14. Hopewell, *Congregation*, 55–56.
15. Ganzevoort, "Narrative Approaches," 221.
16. Hauerwas and Jones, *Why Narrative*, 255.

necessity. Stories hold us together and keep us apart. We tell stories in order to live.[17]

Self-awareness can drastically shape the effect of narratives told within congregations. While congregations may be willing to acknowledge parts of their history where they would see themselves in the wrong, this often comes at the point of a public fallout or a significant church split.[18] Ammerman and Williams suggest that a narrative frame may be especially useful in understanding lived religion and offer three complementary methods of data gathering that are especially suited to exploring religion in its everyday manifestations.[19] Researchers should focus on lived religion and everyday stories to understand religious traditions, beliefs, and times of unsettling change. Further, narrative interviews should be tailored to the audience and cultural institutions, allowing for a more nuanced understanding of religion. Visual methods can also transform research on religion by introducing new dimensions and conceptual categories. Oral diaries and time diaries can help researchers understand everyday activities and patterns of life, bridging cultural differences and fostering intimacy between researchers and participants.[20]

---

17. Anderson and Foley, *Mighty Stories*, 130.

18. For example, in Canada, there is nearly universal recognition among churches which participated in residential schools of the negative nature of these schools. However, in many cases, this came from the public hearing of voices that significantly altered the established narrative. Another example comes from cases where an organization first defends a leader against accusations, only to later revise their narrative once new voices are heard. These examples help to demonstrate that self-awareness for communities of faith and Christian organizations goes beyond growth and organizational health into protecting individuals from abuse at the hands of the organization. An understanding of communal identity will certainly not by itself prevent abusive behavior. These issues run deeper than a lack of self-awareness. However, these examples invoke a lack of organizational self-awareness to demonstrate the problematic nature of having narratives shaped only by those in power.

19. Ammerman and Williams, "Speaking of Methods."

20. Williams, "Constructing a Calling," written by a member of the aforementioned research team, explores the concept of a calling among evangelical Christian international students in the United States. The research used a narrative approach, focusing on the purchase of religious and spiritual narratives in analyzing experience, meaning, identity, and action. The study found that 78 percent of participants connected their faith to their professional aspirations, and all refer to their future career as a calling or part of "God's plan." The study also explored the consequences of a calling in the everyday lives of study participants under three headings: interpreting the past, navigating the present, and finding meaning in the future.

Providing a narrative from multiple sources at various levels of membership will help to shape a narrative which includes various voices. The stories that shape human understanding of experience help to interpret the language used in sharing the messages of the Christian church. This also works in reverse. Through applying the narrative approach to congregational stories, underlying assumptions may be revealed and marginalized voices may speak into the story. Through the interaction of the narrative method within the various narratives at play, narrative research becomes a helpful tool to reveal useful realities of ecclesiological practice.

Within a narrative approach, the story is continually unfolding. The narrative is shaped by the actions of those within the story, by those who tell the story, and by those to whom the story is told. According to Carr, "A community exists where a narrative account exists of a *we* which persists through its experiences and actions. Such an account exists when it gets articulated or formulated—perhaps by only one or a few of the group's members—by reference to the we and is accepted or subscribed to by others."[21]

There are many different voices bringing both complementary and differing opinions on the nature of the narrative approach within practical theology. Through the various strands of these different approaches, several common themes are tied together. A particular theme which emerges is the narrative form of redemptive history, human experience, and community history. The narrative story which is painted by God involves human interaction and is situated within human history. In this aspect, there is a divine invitation to reshape storytelling and the rituals which move out of these stories. Through the integration of worship and pastoral care, the connection between the divine and personal narrative can become clearer.[22] It is in this way that the communal role of narrative may be helpful in fostering congregational practice-led research within communities of faith.

Narrative Interviews

Interviews are an essential component of narrative inquiry and form the key piece of narrative research in this book. They provide extensive and detailed information about a person's experiences, perspectives, and emotions. Through interviews, researchers can collect data that can be used to create a narrative that captures the essence of an individual's or community's

---

21. Carr, "Narrative," 130.
22. Anderson and Foley, *Mighty Stories*, 130.

story. As a result, interviews are an indispensable method for narrative research and are used to investigate complex social and cultural phenomena.

Jeong-Hee Kim provides several valuable insights into effective interviewing for narrative studies. She encourages the interviewer to foster personal stories embedded in social contexts "for those stories reveal how individuals perceive, organize, and give meaning to their understandings of themselves, their experiences, and the world."[23] She also encourages giving space to the interviewee to flesh out metanarratives by allowing long answers to form and avoiding interruptions. By doing so, the interviewer can gain a deeper understanding of the interviewee's perspectives and experiences. This approach can also lead to more insightful and nuanced discussions that go beyond surface-level responses.[24] The environment which an interviewee is in will also influence their experiences and perspectives. This is also shaped by the level of comfort which an interviewee has with their surroundings. In particular, within issues of congregational identity, the presence of other members of the community of faith may shape the narrative which is presented by an interviewee. Therefore, it is important to create a comfortable and safe environment for interviewees to share their experiences and perspectives. Additionally, conducting interviews with individuals in isolation may provide a more accurate representation of their personal beliefs and experiences within the community. For this reason, the interviews for this book have been conducted on a one-on-one basis.

Saturation Point

Within narrative research, the goal is to reach a sample size that meets the saturation point. This is the point at which no new information or themes emerge from the data analysis, even when additional data is added to the sample. Reaching saturation ensures that the researcher has gathered a comprehensive understanding of the phenomenon being studied and can draw meaningful conclusions from the data. It produces a rich and in-depth exploration of individuals' experiences, perspectives, and stories. Within narrative interviews, saturation occurs when new interview data no longer contributes novel insights, but instead validates or duplicates existing findings. It also occurs within a single interview, when the interviewee has

---

23. Kim, *Understanding Narrative Inquiry*, 168.
24. Kim, *Understanding Narrative Inquiry*, 154–83.

shared all the pertinent stories they intend to.[25] At this point, saturation indicates that the researcher has gathered a sufficient amount of information to address the research questions and objectives. It signifies that further interviews may not provide any substantial new knowledge or perspectives. Researchers can then focus on analyzing the collected data and drawing meaningful conclusions from it.

For narrative research that involves an organization such as a community of faith, complications often arise when trying to reach saturation.

> In reality there are practical constraints on the researcher in terms of unforeseen participant attrition (Tuckett, 2004) and in terms of time and resources (Green and Thorogood, 2004). This is particularly important as there are arguments relating to saturation and quality within each interview and, therefore, researchers need to pay attention to both the length of interviews as well as the number of interviews (Onwuegbuzie and Leech, 2005). Transparency about these limitations on reaching saturation does not necessarily invalidate the findings. If saturation is not reached this simply means that the phenomenon has not yet been fully explored rather than that the findings are invalid (Morse, 1995). It is acceptable, therefore, that any limitations of sampling adequacy are transparently reported. Researchers thus need to be clear in dissemination if they reached saturation, how they reached it and what issues they faced during recruitment.[26]

Therefore, if saturation is not fully reached, this does not invalidate the data acquired. Instead, it highlights the need for further exploration and potential limitations in the study's sample size or recruitment process. It is crucial for researchers to acknowledge these limitations and provide a transparent account of their efforts to achieve saturation in order to ensure the credibility and reliability of their findings. This transparency allows for a more comprehensive understanding of the research process and enhances the credibility of the findings. Additionally, acknowledging challenges faced during recruitment can provide valuable insights for future studies and contribute to the advancement of knowledge in the field.

---

25. Suárez-Ortega, "Performance."
26. O'Reilly and Parker, "Unsatisfactory Saturation," 193–94.

Role of Narrator

When presenting the narratives of the churches, it is important to acknowledge that I, as the narrator, come into this with my own biases, views, and opinions. Reflexivity is referred to as "the constant awareness, assessment, and reassessment by the researcher of the researcher's own contribution/influence/shaping of intersubjective research and the consequent research findings."[27] As explored particularly in chapter 1, this work emerges from my own practice while also taking a "step back." This allows research to emerge not in denial of personal influence but with understanding and ongoing assessment of it.

IDENTIFICATION WITH AN ORGANIZATIONAL GROUP SCALE (IWOGS)

This research contains, in addition to the narrative interview, a survey which went out to church attendees. This survey draws on the work of Mael and Tetrick.[28] Identification with a psychological group or organization (IDPG) is defined by these authors as the perception of sharing a focal group's experiences and sharing group members' characteristics. IDPG differs from organizational commitment empirically and overlaps less with commitment than job satisfaction, organizational satisfaction, and job involvement.

Variants of this survey tool have been used in many studies across disciplines, with over 250 peer-reviewed works citing this study. This article served as the foundation for developing a matrix for social identity research in a variety of fields. For example, in the study of political science, a multi-item partisan identity scale was proposed as a more accurate predictor of campaign participation than a strong stance on subjectively important policy issues, ideological self-positioning, or ideological identity. This study demonstrated the connection between an expressive partisan identity that drives campaign participation and intense emotional reactions to ongoing campaign events.[29]

In a recent study published in the *Journal of Social and Personal Relationships*, this scale was used to explore how college students' sense of social dominance, social positions, prosocial obligation, and sense of

---

27 Salzman, "On Reflexivity," 806.
28. Mael and Tetrick, "Identifying Organizational Identification."
29. Huddy et al., "Expressive Partisanship."

belongingness affected their prosocial behavior between groups across age, gender, race/ethnicity, and department affiliation.[30] Another study in the field of business ethics utilized this scale. This study examined how a follower's identification with a leader and an organization influences the follower's integrity of behavior and organizational citizenship.[31]

This scale has not been used extensively in studies of religious congregations.[32] The 2001 article "Antecedents of Member Commitment to the Local Church"[33] utilized a mail survey to a large congregation to determine that participation in small groups was an important antecedent of commitment to the congregation. This survey, while sharing some similarities to the IDPG scale, was actually adapted from the earlier work of Mowday et al.,[34] which was likewise drawn upon by the 1992 Mael and Tetrick study. There have, however, been many uses of the IDPG scale in studies of organizational identity, including organizations which contain various levels of leaders, such as business organizations.[35]

The use of this organizational group scale does not represent an independent method separate from the method of narrative inquiry, but rather a data collection tool under the wider scope of the narrative method. While this data collection tool is not used primarily within narrative studies, this provides an excellent resource to produce meaningful data on communal identity as one piece of data collection.

RECRUITMENT PROCESS AND ETHICAL CONSIDERATIONS

Within narrative inquiry, it is essential to examine potential conflicts of interest. The churches who participated in this study were all a part of The Christian Missionary Alliance in Canada (C&MA), the same denomination in which I hold my ordination. No congregation which has employed

---

30. Xiao et al., "Young Adults' Behavior."
31. Ete et al., "Behavioral Integrity."
32. One exception is Patrikios, "Self-Stereotyping." However, this study is focused primarily on intersectionality of evangelicalism and republicanism, and as such is not particularly relevant to this study. I do not include this here as the study was focused on the political identity, not on the role of identity within communities of faith.
33. Bond, "Antecedents."
34. Mowday et al., "Measurement."
35. Ete et al., "Behavioral Integrity."

or appointed me in a leadership role was involved, to avoid a perceived pastor-congregant relationship. I also have no direct authority over any congregations or church leaders with which I have conducted research. Potential conflicts of interest were also minimized through clear communication of the researcher's role. For example, when interviewing a church leader who belongs to my own denomination, I clearly stated that I was not interviewing in my role as a worker in the denomination. Participants were informed that I do not conduct research as a pastor or on behalf of a denomination. Appropriate boundaries were also established during researcher-participant interactions. This would mean that, for conversations involving faith and church involvement, I did not act within interviews as a practitioner but instead, if necessary, referred participants to counselling resources.

This book required several stages of consent:

1. The appropriate church leader gave written permission for recruitment and observational data collection.
2. Survey participants gave consent prior to entering survey through selecting "yes."
3. Survey participants were invited following the completion of the survey to be contacted for an interview. To preserve anonymity of the survey, this was given in the form of a link to a separate survey.
4. Interview participants consented using a survey sent via Zoom chat, and the researcher was available to answer any questions.

The participants were able to stop taking the survey at any time and not submit their results, but they were not able to withdraw their survey after completion due to it being an anonymous survey. Interview participants could withdraw their consent up to one month following an interview.

Church leaders were approached via email, telephone, or in-person to inquire about participation. Upon agreement of a church to participate, the church leadership was asked to send the survey and script via email with a paper option available to the congregants via internal congregational communication (email lists, etc.). To preserve the privacy of the congregants, contact information was kept private from the researcher. At the end of the survey, a link was sent to a separate survey where participants were invited to provide their contact information so as to be contacted for a follow-up interview. Churches had an opportunity to opt out of the interview phase and only participate in the survey stage. At no point did a pastor or church leader directly conduct the survey.

Preserving anonymity is challenging when a project requires comprehensive participant descriptions and discussions of related research contexts. There is a possibility of breaching confidentiality if the characteristics and experiences of individuals become recognizable in research reports, even when pseudonyms are used. This situation is referred to as deductive disclosure.[36] In the present project, the risk of deductive disclosure has been reduced through a number of processes. Pseudonyms were used for churches, towns, and individuals. The only case where individuals are named involves references to individuals who are both public figures and not directly involved within the study. Individuals who were interviewed were not asked to keep their responses confidential, as that was not necessary to maintain the integrity of the study nor was it practical with the nature of the study. However, as a researcher, I kept all responses strictly confidential.

The term *member* will be used to describe these individuals. However, this is unrelated to membership in a church's structural capacity. Interviewees may include those who attend the church but are not members in a structural sense. Membership, here, refers to belonging to the community of the church rather than in a formal, structural sense.

STUDY PARTICIPANTS

Four churches participated in the survey, totalling sixty-two people. The chart below depicts the churches and the information associated with their participants. Pseudonyms are used for all church names, and these are Riverdale Alliance Church, Archet Church, Koradai Alliance Church, and Kamino Alliance Church. Kamino was the only church that did not participate in the interview phase. The responses from Kamino were helpful in adding additional comparative data. However, for the purposes of this study, no report is presented on Kamino due to the lack of narrative data. To ensure that the most useful data emerges, the generations of Gen Z and Millennial have been combined in comparative charts used in the dissemination of data.

The initial collection took place in a survey of four churches which included participation from leadership and congregations. These surveys

36. Kaiser, "Protecting Respondent Confidentiality."

included collectively sixty-two participants across the four churches. While the intake of participating churches was in principle open to all Christian denominations, only those within the Alliance denomination ended up participating. This could potentially limit the scope and diversity of the research findings, but it also allows for a more focused and specific analysis of a particular group within the larger Christian community. The limited scope of this research also allows for a thicker description to emerge. While research projects such as Ammerman and Williams focus on wider society affiliation, this particular research focuses on the self-awareness of collective identities of particular churches. The research pool being limited to Alliance churches allows for a more focused and in-depth analysis of the self-awareness of collective identities within these specific churches. Furthermore, as a practitioner within The Alliance Canada, I have awareness around issues which emerged. At the same time, however, this focus limits the ability of the study to provide comparative analysis based on denominational affiliation and various traditions. In addition, this limits the ability of the study to examine practices outside of the C&MA as they relate to communal belonging. This is a limit of this study. However, in a study of four churches, a deeper, thick description may be more beneficial, and this is enhanced through the common denominational affiliation found in this study. This study is also limited in scope to predominantly white churches, and out of the three churches interviewed, only one church leader was a visible minority. In addition, there will be blind spots in exploring complexities related to certain subgroup identities due to my own lack of experience with belonging to the relevant marginalized groups (e.g., women, ethnic minorities, etc.).

A limit of this study is that only participants currently a part of a church were surveyed or interviewed. Therefore, the findings may not be representative of the views and experiences of those who do not attend church or have left the church. Future research could expand the sample to include a more diverse range of participants to provide a more comprehensive understanding of the topic. Barriers to belonging are certainly not an exclusive reason for people choosing to not attend a particular church, and many community members may cite different religious affiliation or a number of other factors as the reason they do not want to participate in a church community. However, what would be relevant to this study is to speak to community members who would agree with a statement such as "I would be apart of <church community> if it were not for x," or "If x, I would join <church community>."

Despite the interest in obtaining such data, it was not feasible within this particular research project due to ethical considerations, the scope of research, and recruitment limitations. Given the nature of the topic of belonging in a church, contacting former members or those outside of the church may risk upsetting or traumatizing them. Because the recruitment for this research was through local churches, an invitation to participate in a survey which came from a church may not be received well to those who do not feel they belong. The scope of this research is focused on congregational self-awareness of their own identity, and as such data collected within the church remains valuable for exploring this. While this particular study is not able to explore such areas, it is my hope that future projects will emerge. For example, a wide-reaching research study could be done on a particular town, including attendees of churches and non-attendees. Comparative research in these areas could be done then, on perceived barriers of entry from congregations, church leadership, and those outside the church. Alternatively, a study could be done on former members of a particular church using this method.

ETHNICITY OF PARTICIPANTS

To protect the anonymity of the participants, some specific data pertaining to ethnicity has not be shown relating to the churches identified. The majority of those participated identified as white or similar (e.g., Caucasian, European, British, etc.). Fifteen percent either declined to answer or wrote answers which did not define a specific ethnicity (e.g., "Canadian"). Finally, 7 percent included the following answers: "visual minority," "Indian," and "African." In order to preserve the anonymity of these individuals, these results are grouped together as "People of Color."[37]

These results do not accurately reflect the ethnicity of the church attendees but rather represent the sample size. Notably, every church during the interview phase reported the presence of people of color in their congregation, yet only one church's surveys reported on this. Due to the small sample size of various ethnicities, the comparative data presented will not

---

37. The reason for this grouping is not to imply that these ethnicities are a monolith, but rather to pull usable data from this smaller sample size without containing identifying information.

be as strong as other categories. Interestingly, there was an underrepresentation of participation in non-white participants for every church except for one. While there was not enough significant data to determine the cause of this variance, it is worth noting that the church with the strongest results was the only church interviewed which had a pastoral leader who was a visible minority.

A notable weakness of the survey data is the lack of diversity in ethnicity in order to provide more extensive comparative data. However, some potentially interesting data can be found in the results. Overall, there was a net reduction in identification with the community of the church for people of color. A further (predictable) finding is that members of color are less convinced than white members that their church reflects the diversity of the surrounding community.

There is a negative difference in seeing oneself as an outsider for people of color as opposed to white respondents. Those who were people of color felt less often like outsiders than white respondents. This trend is not explained by the specific church these participants attended, as this church on average feels like an outsider more often than the total average. While there is not enough of a sample size to fully explore this, it is an interesting anomaly within this data.

QUANTITATIVE CONSIDERATIONS

As a qualitative study exploring the usefulness of these tools for church leaders, the sample size of survey participants was sufficient to allow the survey to provide a glimpse into the subgroup identities of these congregations and their relative influence on belonging for those who participated. As with any collection of data from a subgroup (that is, those who took the survey), further participation would have allowed a more nuanced and holistic snapshot of the intergroup identities. However, this sample size was sufficient in being able to produce useful comparative data on respondents from these congregations. It should be kept in mind that the primary goal of the present study was to explore the potential usefulness of SIT for church leaders, rather than to provide a comprehensive and accurate description of any particular church.

The interview sample sizes and survey sample sizes varied dramatically between participating churches. Riverdale had the largest consistent sample size between surveys and interviews, as well as the largest participation overall in the narrative research. Archet and Koradai provided a much lower interview sample at three interviews each, as opposed to eleven interviews from Riverdale. While attempts were made to promote further engagement (through church administration sending out an additional reminder), no further participation was gained. The participation from these churches enabled development of congregational narratives; however, these narratives had limitations that did not affect my study of Riverdale. In particular, there were areas of Archet church's survey results in which the lack of narrative data prevented further insights from being gleaned, as is discussed in chapter 4. Koradai was particularly limited in developing data on the early history of the church; however, the extensive narrative data provided by those who participated allowed me to produce a significantly more extensive narrative than with Archet.

It is important to highlight that the goal of this research is not to produce empirical theology through analysis of quantitative data. The above participation allowed this project to proceed in providing a qualitative study on the usefulness of these tools in enhancing the self-awareness of church leadership in congregational identity. The IWOGS scale in particular provides a snapshot view of comparative data of congregants solely as a resource for the qualitative research that is at the center of this book.

SUMMARY OF RESEARCH PHASES

Phase One

As noted above, the survey in this research draws on the work of Mael and Tetrick.[38] This survey took approximately five to ten minutes to complete and involved questions regarding belonging and the congregational, intergroup, and personal identity according to individuals in churches. This survey was sent out to congregants, including church members and leaders, with the aforementioned ethical considerations. This survey was conducted using LimeSurvey.

---

38. Mael and Tetrick, "Identifying Organizational Identification."

Research Scope

Survey Questions

Question	Options
Categorization Questions	
Birth Year	Text Input Prefer not to say
Thinking about your background, what ethnicity you consider yourself?	Text Input Prefer not to say
Were you born in Canada?	Yes No Prefer not to say
Marital Status	Single Married Divorced Common Law Prefer not to say
Gender	Text Input Prefer not to say
Which best describes your role in <church name> (check all that apply)	Church member or affiliate Board / Elder member Ministry staff Volunteer ministry leadership Other None of the above Prefer not to say
Group Identity Questions	
For how many years have you attended <church name>?	Under 1 Year 1–2 years 3–5 years 6–10 years 11–20 years 21–29 years Over 30 years (Prefer not to say)

How important is being a part of <church name> to you?	Not important Somewhat important Important Very important I don't know
To what extent do you consider yourself an insider with respect to the community of <church name>?	Scale of 1–5, 1 being on the outside looking in, 5 being on the inside looking in
When you speak of the <church name> community, how often do you use "we" instead of "they"?	Never Rarely Sometimes Often Always
When you think of <church name>, do you feel you are an integral part of that community?	Yes No
How often do you see yourself as an outsider in <church name>?	Never Rarely Sometimes Often Always
To what extent to you agree / disagree with the following statements:	
I feel our church leadership is aware of the identity of <church name>	1–5
I feel <church name>'s identity is aligned with my own identity.	1–5
<church name> reflects the diversity of the surrounding community.	1–5
<church name> is open to diversity of Christian beliefs.	1–5
Does <church name> offer services in other languages?	No Yes I Don't Know
Is being a part of <church name> a central part of your identity?	Never Rarely Sometimes Often Always
Is your faith a central part of your identity?	Never Rarely Sometimes Often Always

How important is it to you to attend a church of your denomination?	Not important Somewhat important Important Very Important
What is the likelihood you would you attend a church of a different denomination?	Scale 1–5
How welcoming to outsiders do you feel <church name> is?	Scale 1–10
How difficult would it be to leave <church name>?	Scale 1–10
How far do you live from <church name>'s meeting space?	Under 2 KM 2–5 KM 5–10 KM 10–20 KM 20–30 KM Over 30 KM
In which type of gatherings do you feel you are an integral part of <church name>?	Small groups Weekly worship service Informal meetings with church members Church dinners Ministry teams Prayer groups Other None of the above

Table 1: Survey Questions

Phase Two

For the second data collection, church members, including church leaders, were invited to participate in a follow-up interview conducted by the researcher. Seventeen participants agreed to participate in these follow-up interviews. These participants included eleven from Riverdale Alliance Church, three from Koradai Alliance Church, and three from Archet Church. These sessions took approximately from one half to one hours and were taken utilizing audio recording with observations being journaled using a word processor. These interviews took place on Zoom or in person at the church's place of worship. They focused directly on the narratives of identity which existed in the communities of faith and factors which surrounded church identity and utilized the methodology of narrative inquiry.

Interview Script

Through the tools of narrative inquiry, I sought to gain a deeper understanding of how individuals experience and interpret their sense of (non-)belonging in relation to a particular Christian congregation. In these narrative interviews, I sought to uncover nuanced and insightful perspectives that went beyond surface-level responses. These interviews aimed to contribute to a greater understanding of the role of communal identity within these communities of faith and how individuals perceive communal identity in relation to their own sense of belonging. Below is the script used for these interviews.

- Hello, my name is Paul Lucas. Thank you for agreeing to participate in this interview. Just to remind you, I'm looking at opinions about church identity and belonging. Interviews will be one-to-one and will be open-ended (not just "yes or no" answers). Because of this, the exact wording may change a little. Sometimes I will use other short questions to make sure I understand what you told me, if I need more information when we are talking, or to learn what you think or feel about something. These include "So, you are saying that . . . ?" and "Why do you think that is . . . ?" or "Please tell me more."
- How long have you attended <church name>? How would you describe your role in your church?
- How would you describe <church name>'s identity?
- Can you think of a time that comes to your mind where you felt that you really belonged in a church community? It could be any community, not necessarily one you currently attend.
- Can you think of a time where you felt you did not belong in a church community? How open do you feel your community of faith is to newcomers?
- Do you think your church could be doing anything more to lower barriers of entry to those outside of your community of faith?
- How do you feel your community of faith's identity aligns with your own? Are there ways it does not?
- Is there anything about your background, identity, or anything else that causes you to feel like an outsider in your church?

- Are there certain programs or events which make you feel especially part of the community? Are there any particular programs or events which you feel were designed for someone else?
- What does it mean for <church name> to be a welcoming community?
- There are some people who believe that a church should prioritize being a close-knit community, and others who believe the priority should be being open to outsiders. If you were to choose one as the highest priority, which way would you lean?
- We have spoken about openness and being a welcome community. Do you think there are times where it is appropriate for a church to be exclusive?
- One thing I noticed in the survey results was _____. Does this survey data reflect your understanding of the congregation? Do you have any insight as to why that might be?
- Is there anything we forgot or is there something important that we should know about identity and belonging in your community of faith?

Phase Three

The third phase involved presenting anonymized data to church leaders and then inviting their feedback. This feedback was crucial, providing an opportunity for church leaders to offer suggestions or make any necessary adjustments before I finalized the analyses of the three churches. Also, it allowed me to observe how the research data did or did not help them as church leaders to better understand the identities of their congregations and the experiences of their community members as regards communal belonging.

First, church leaders were walked through a brief overview of the research. This not only allowed the church leaders to have deeper insight into the data but also provided useful feedback in communication of complex social psychology in a way that is useful and meaningful to church leaders. Additionally, church leaders were given the opportunity to ask questions and seek clarification on the overview of the research. This allowed myself to see which areas were unclear and which areas connected with the needs of church leaders.

Next, the church leaders were presented with the anonymized data. This data included key findings that highlighted trends and patterns within the church community. This would include both the survey and interview material. During this time, the church leaders were asked for reactions to data and invited to ask clarifying questions. The church leaders' reactions and questions provided valuable insights into their understanding of the research findings and helped identify any gaps in their knowledge. Additionally, this interactive session fostered open dialogue and collaboration between the researchers and church leaders, enabling a deeper exploration of the implications and potential actions based on the data.

Finally, the church leaders were invited to reflect through a few questions which are listed below, which helped to assess the strengths and weaknesses of this research as it relates to the usefulness of SIT and narrative inquiry for church leaders. These questions included inquiries about the practical application of the findings within their specific church context, potential barriers or challenges which have been discovered, and any additional information or resources they felt would be helpful in further understanding and utilizing the research. These questions included:

- Was there anything that surprised you from this presentation? If so, please describe.
- Do you feel you have a greater awareness of your communal identity from this presentation?
- Do you feel that the narrative presented differs from your own understanding of the narrative of <church name>?
- Could you describe your reaction to this presentation?
- What new questions have arisen as a result of this presentation?
- Are there ways that this presentation was beneficial to <church name>?
- Are there any additional comments you have around this presentation and study?

This reflective exercise enabled valuable feedback and insights from the church leaders. By gathering feedback and insights from church leaders, I was able to gain a deeper understanding of how the findings of this research could be practically applied in their church contexts. This data is not helpful in self-awareness if the data produced is not understood by church

Research Scope

leaders. Therefore, the data must be clear enough for church leaders to be able to glean insight on their congregations. This feedback in phase three was helpful in providing reflection on improvements in these areas.

CHAPTER 4

Research Data

THIS CHAPTER WILL PRESENT the data gathered during the three aforementioned research phases. The data will be analyzed and interpreted to gain insight into the research questions and objectives. Any limitations or challenges encountered during the data collection process will also be addressed. This represents the narrative profiles and identity mapping that were gathered during the research. The collected data will be analyzed to identify patterns, trends, and relationships within the narrative profiles and identity mapping. This will allow for a better understanding of the participants' experiences and perspectives.

RIVERDALE ALLIANCE CHURCH

Riverdale Alliance Church is an average-sized church in a small town in Ontario, Canada. What follows is the narrative profile developed through the phases of research. It is important to note that the statistical data represent statistics from the sample size, not from the actual congregation, as this research was limited to those who participated in surveys and in interviews.

Demographic Statistics of Riverdale Alliance Church

Survey respondents included those in the age range of Baby Boomers (36 percent), Gen X (29 percent), Millennials (14 percent), and War Kids (21 percent), with no Gen Z respondents. Participants were 71 percent female and 29 percent male. Once again, this does not represent the actual gender makeup of the congregation, but rather the makeup of those who participated in the survey. All participants from Riverdale (who identified their ethnicity) identified as white, European, Caucasian, or other similar categories. According to interviews, there are some who attend who are visible minorities, but the congregation is predominately white. Pastor John[1] stated that the church is predominately white, stating the demographics of survey respondents "probably represents the church, other than ethnicity. . . . If I had to do the math, we could have like 8–10 percent who are visibly non-Caucasian."

Denominational Affiliation

Out of the interviewees, most did not express a history with the denomination as a factor in their choosing RAC. The survey data showed a wide range of degrees of affiliation.[2] As will be explored below, the church has had a complicated history as it relates to their denominational affiliation. Pastor John stated that this matched what he observed in the church, stating, "You could arguably say there has not been a lot of denominational connection over the last number of years and [there was] pushing for a more independent congregational identity." There did seem to be a shift in recent history towards a deeper denominational affiliation. Several interviewers described Pastor John as "very Alliance" and felt that the church was moving to be more connected with the Alliance. This came in a variety of ways, in particular through Pastor John referring in sermons and conversations to areas which influence Alliance identity.[3] In this, there was a

---

1. Within my own practice, although I am an ordained minister, I am very rarely referred to as "Reverend Paul," usually called simply by my name or "Pastor Paul." This practice is relatively common in other Alliance churches that I have seen and, during the interviews, the pastors were referenced either by their first name or "Pastor <first name>." I make this clarification to say that I use these terms interchangeably, and no further inference should be made to inclusion and exclusion of these titles in these reports.

2. A possible misunderstanding in the questions may have emerged from confusion over the permanence of what attending a church implied. In hindsight, it may have been more precise to ask if someone would "permanently join" or "become a part" rather than attend, as attending could mean to some regular attendance and to others attending a single service such as with friends. Nonetheless, the degree to denominational affiliation reflected in the survey is consistent with the interview results, with a range from high affiliation to low affiliation.

3. A related interesting study is Ward, "Sermons," which explores aspects of

push towards making involvement in the Alliance much more central to congregational identity. This is closely linked with the contextual identity of being independent as a church moving towards trivialization and an emphasis of the identity of the Alliance denomination. This represents an identity differentiation between the past and present church—in particular leadership—through the comparative fit of having a pastor now with strong Alliance ties following (notwithstanding transitional leadership) a pastor with no Alliance background.

Reasons for Joining

When asked what brought them to Riverdale Community Church (RAC), most participants immediately shared stories of what brought them to the town of Riverdale. Some participants required an additional prompt to share why they chose to attend RAC specifically, whereas other participants moved into sharing why they chose RAC. Many participants, including those who had attended for the longest periods and those who were very involved in church oversight, did not express a long-time connection with the community of Riverdale. All participants interviewed did not grow up at RAC as children. The findings from the interviews and surveys were fairly consistent on this, with the majority of the survey respondents having attended six to twenty years. Of the survey respondents, 61.5 percent lived ten kms or under from the church's meeting space, which is fairly consistent with the interviewee's reports. There was a variety of answers from interviewees as to why they originally chose Riverdale Alliance Church and why they chose to stay. The factor for most interviewees in coming to RAC was its programs for youth and children. Other interviewees cited preaching style, proximity to home, and feeling drawn by God. Many interviewees cited a sense of calling as a factor in staying at RAC. Others cited the friendly environment, connection with members, and a belief in the programs and missions of the church. Generally, the trend among interviewees was that practical factors initially drew them to RAC, with spiritual and interpersonal factors causing them to remain part of the congregation.

---

identification, gender, and power within the context of sermons. The method of this study is based on the work of Ashforth and Mael, "Social Identity Theory," which relies on SIT.

Research Data

Narratives of Church History

The following represents shared narrative history collected through interviews. Within the narrative history shared, there emerged several key themes in the history of Riverdale which form the following subheadings.

Formation Narratives

Approximately forty years ago, a small group of people founded RAC. The church was established following a schism with the Baptist Church located nearby. This Baptist Church has also fractured since the formation of other churches RAC mistakenly entered their denomination. The initial pastor had no affiliation with the denomination. When the individual went to file or register the Church with the denomination, they became affiliated with the Alliance denomination instead. According to one member, "It always kind of makes me chuckle, but at the same time I sense that, until currently, that has actually been a good descriptor of RAC." Since then, Riverdale has experienced significant expansion, and RAC has endured difficult periods throughout its history. A member who had been there since the beginning reportedly stated that RAC's history is "not a good story." Through the years, pastors have been described as having brief tenures and being new to pastoring. According to one member, "The church has been very hard on its pastors, and every one of them that has left has left on not good terms. . . . [I] think that people don't look at the pastor as the Lord's anointed. They look at the pastor as their employee that they can use and manipulate. And I think that's not a good thing. That's not a good thing." Another member remarked, "I don't remember anything specific as a bad thing that happened, but just that the pastors that came, didn't do what they were supposed to do, I guess, I don't know. But there was probably still unrest in the church anyway. And probably a pastor didn't have much of a chance."

One individual commented on a pastor who became very ill, although little more was said on this issue. There were founding members of the church who were said to be "extremely legalistic and negative" and who disrupted annual meetings. When this narrative was shared with the pastor, John reflected, "Yeah, that would follow the common narrative I've heard. . . . I think you're tracking with the general theme." John's agreement with the common narrative suggests that he is familiar with similar stories and experiences. He believed the shared narrative aligns well with the overarching message or pattern he has encountered before.

As the interviews unfolded, the diverse perspectives and experiences of these individuals within the RAC came to light. Each person added a unique hue to the intricate tapestry of the church; their lives were intertwined in the pursuit of faith and belonging. Their stories illuminated the challenges, joys, and hopes that resonated within the walls of RAC, fostering a vibrant and diverse community of believers. While those interviewed did not have a lifelong history in the community, there was a deep desire present to engage in a church that was within the community they lived in. James described the desire to be involved in the community, saying, "We made a very conscious decision that we were going to find a local church. You know, it was. We could have travelled back and forth for forty minutes each time to our preexisting church. But we want to make a difference in our community. We want to be involved in our community. And going to a local church is important." Similarly, George commented, "I've been attending the church here ever since [retiring and moving]. It was the closest church to my house, the closest evangelical church to my house, so, okay. It's only a few minutes away. So it was just the proximity." Many also communicated a spiritual sense of the Holy Spirit calling them to engage in this church.

Pastoral History

In the midst of these issues, there was one pastor that several members spoke favorably of. In addition, all interviewees spoke very favorably about the current pastor. While there is admittedly the risk of participants being overly positive about those currently in power due to power structures, participants were very honest in general about previous and current leadership. According to one member, a previous pastor was also extremely affable and compassionate. "He was a good shepherd." Another member stated, "The first Sunday that we listened to [redacted], my husband connected with him. And that was a big factor for me, knowing that he was a great pastor, and we just felt very welcome. And so we just continued on, and my husband was saved in that church under [redacted]."

After this pastor left and was replaced, there was a period of unrest, which one member described as a very bad period in which many people left. One person described this as people turning against the pastor, while most described individuals becoming victims of spiritual abuse under the leadership of a pastor. Some individuals began to notice behavior that was seen as spiritually abusive and found, through reporting it, a lack of accountability in leadership structures. Another member described this time: "There was definitely spiritual abuse happening, and we were on the verge of becoming very legalistic."

One person who approached church leadership about issues stated,

> I did not feel heard within; at times I was not welcomed, and it felt like I was causing trouble. If I had just been quiet, it would've been better. And the only reason that we persevered and kind of stuck through that was that there were a lot of people that were getting hurt that probably didn't have the spiritual background that we did.

One member reported speaking to their spouse as they saw the church going through this time and predicting the pastor was going to resign a few weeks before he announced his resignation. This period was, for most interviewees, a very significant time in the church's history and, for most who were interviewed, an extremely negative time. During this time, participants described "spiritual abuse." Although this was not solely directed at women, a number of participants expressed that women were the primary victims of this spiritual abuse. For the female interviewees who attended at this time, the salience of their subgroup identity as women increased through the comparative fit of seeing a difference between their current leadership and the previous one. It is not just the actions or traits of the pastor that are being referenced as salient; rather, it is these women's identities as women who affirmed the importance of female leadership. As this pastor emphasized a congregational identity which saw women as unable to lead, their differentiation within the community increased and their sense of belonging decreased.

Misogyny and Abuse

According to one member,

> There has been a significant thread of misogyny in the church's history. This has resulted in spiritual abuse and victimization of many people, particularly women. Trying to understand the depth of the hurt and wounding caused by this systemic misogyny is difficult. It's also challenging for the church leaders who were

supposed to protect their congregation but were unaware of the level of abuse. How do you unpack and address such profound damage? It's a question I grapple with often.

There are several issues which to many in the church have seemed intertwined, though some may see them as separate. One issue is the theological position of the role of women in ministry. Another issue is the treatment of women within the church. Another is the reality of abusive leadership from those in power. For many people in the church, they saw these realities coming together in a very difficult way in recent years. One member stated, "What I've realized is that benevolent patriarchy is just a nicer-looking cage because it can turn so quickly from benevolent to abusive." In prior years, this did not seem to be a salient issue, although my research did not bring any information on this particular issue prior to the mid-1990s. However, there is ongoing confusion, inconsistency, and lack of communication on this issue.

Confusion and Change in Gender Roles

Through the history of Riverdale Alliance, there was a lack of clarity regarding women's roles.[4] Complementarian churches may have, at times, specific roles which are restricted to men or women. For example, in some churches, women may be prevented from being pastors or elders, but may operate in any other function. For some churches, women may only not be able to have the role of senior pastor. For some, women may not be permitted to preach, whereas other complementarian churches will allow this. These examples are not meant to endorse these practices, but rather to reveal the lack of clarity which could not be provided by the denomination nor by historical precedent. Therefore, misogyny had a place to grow. One person described the progression of a prior pastor as telling women not to bring their Bibles onstage, then saying not to say any verses, then not allowing women to speak on the stage at all. This created surprise from female missionaries who had previously spoken:

---

4. While I have attempted to narrate this section in a neutral matter, my own views as an egalitarian—and also the personal impact of having a wife who works in a pastoral role—have likely influenced my presentation of the narrative. Furthermore, as a man, I have had the privilege of never being inhibited in ministry due to my gender. Despite these unavoidable biases, I have attempted to present the narrative given by interviewees as faithfully as possible.

Research Data

> When the missionaries would come, suddenly the women ... like it had always been, there was always a thing about if it ... don't let the women preach, but you can let them share. But now it became, "Don't even let the women go up there. The women can go down and do a special event with the kids downstairs while the man preaches upstairs." And [redacted] came up to me and she said, "What's going on in your church? Are women not allowed to speak?" And I was just like, "I actually don't know what's going on. I don't know." And so it just became like ... it became kind of a joke, really.

We see here the lack of value given to women causing salient differentiation of women's identity in the time that there was an emphasis of practices which reduced the ability of women to have roles which they previously held.[5]

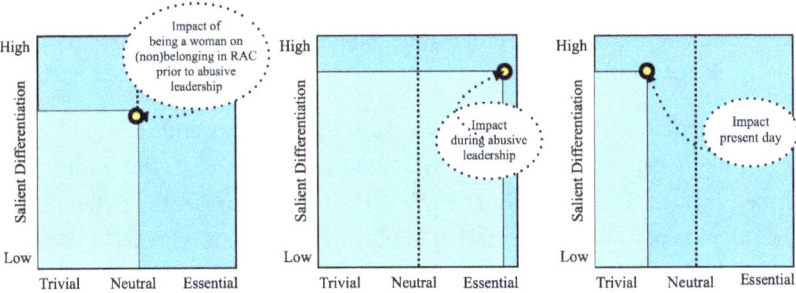

Figure 10: TEST: Women in RAC

Another member spoke of a time where she was taken aback from the inability to speak,

> And it was just like, where's my voice ... where is our voice here? And it was just, it was such a strong and dark attack, and you knew exactly where it's coming from. And I'm dealing with attacks to this day because I know the Lord's working not only in me, but at the church and he wants to use missions and whatever else, and but to feel like you have no voice and it's gotta be up to the men to give you your voice.

---

5. While these changes also had related impact on male members—specifically those who may hold different views on the role of women than leadership, as well as those in close relationship with the affected women—the primary subgroup which was affected by these changes were women at the church.

Several people, one who identified as a "pretty strong complementarian," spoke on this issue as a theological issue, in particular regarding whether women would be permitted as elders and pastors. One person said,

> Over the years, I mean, the church has been fairly conservative, so the complementarian thing is only fairly recent. We struggled with the Alliance. It's, I mean it's old now, the Alliance sort of downloading that whole thing on churches to make the decision [on women in ministry] for themselves.

Another person commented,

> Even though The Alliance Canada back in, 2000 was it, whatever, I forget the dates . . . voted and accepted women to be ordained and to, to minister within churches. And that caused people to leave. Riverdale Community was looking at doing all this transition work and people left because women were going to be able to, not necessarily, or ordain, but you now, the right to speak on a Sunday during a Sunday service.

These responses reflect a drastic lack of clarity in the denominational framework, likely caused by a number of issues, one of which is the undermentioned lack of denominational clarity. They also represent a difference in the salience of a complementarian identity. Participants who self-identified as complementarian were men and emphasized that if changes in this area were to occur, they would no longer feel they belonged in this church. In contrast, when there were changes in these areas, the women interviewed found these changes noticeable as it affected their roles and ability to participate in the church.

These shifts in the church caused not just a restriction on women in leadership roles, but a restriction on women being able to present concerns to leadership. This lack of denominational clarity led to a significant imbalance of power within the church, with women being marginalized and their voices silenced. Pastor John spoke of the manner in which the church has gone beyond even simply adopting a complementarian position, stating, "Even within a 'capital C' complementarian position living out that, living out that theology, what has happened at this church has, has been so far from loving that it's disgusting. . . . I've been told by numerous people that for a while, the identity of being a complementarian group—in the sense of putting down women—was the identity of a number of leadership here." This reflected a movement in the past of the subgroup and congregational identity of "complementarian" moving from trivial to essential. Pastor John emphasized that the church's approach to complementarianism has been taken to an extreme. This "distorted understanding of complementarianism" became the defining characteristic of the church's leadership for a significant period, as shared by multiple individuals. One member stated,

> When you start questioning leadership because you know something's wrong and they refuse to hear you when they, when [we] started to be called gossips, and when we started to be seen as just, you know, as you know, "don't let the women talk!" (nervous laugh) That's when you realize your value is not as important . . . you know, that's a tough feeling.

In this example, this member's sense of her own personal identity aligning with the stereotype she had of the church dramatically shifted when she expected church leadership to take her concerns seriously and found otherwise. Another member summarized this time, saying,

> I would say right now [our identity] is pretty dramatically changing. We did have a transition pastor who came and led us through, so I would say we were on the verge of, well there was definitely spiritual abuse happening and we were on the verge of becoming very, I don't know what denomination it would've been, but a very legalistic one for sure. And then that was kind of called out and, and dealt with and, and so the church then realized we've got deeper problems than simply one part of the leadership. And so took advantage of that, of the transitional team and a transition pastor who helped to work through a lot of things. And what it came down to is basically some main leadership in the church thought the church all agreed with them and they had very, very definite views. You know, tended towards kind of a legalistic, very stuck in just certain theories and beliefs and very much strong complementarian and came to realize in the transition process that were not strong complementarian, not egalitarian yet, but definitely women have a lot more of a role now.

Some members who had left the church at the time of the leadership abuses reported feeling connected with friends at the church in the midst of not being at the church. This represents an interesting subgroup category development where some individuals were not formally part of the church but self-identified as part of the community.[6] There were a number of

---

6. I am not referring to not being formally part of the community in the sense of church attendance or membership, which can range to the degree which one self-identifies as a member. Rather, these individuals intentionally withdrew from the church and

members who returned after a particular pastor resigned. As one person said, "The moment the pastor left, all of a sudden you see these people coming back." This provides an interesting example of a sudden shift in the salient differentiation in a community of faith. While there remained emphasis towards the reduction of women's belonging, the overall move pulled towards neutral. In addition, the absence of this pastor caused the salient differentiation to not disappear, but lessen. Interestingly, these two shifts reflect a very strong shift for women who were affected by changes in their ability to hold certain roles from exclusion to inclusion in a very short season. The prior leader was causing a salient differentiation to rise and promoted that differentiation through emphasis. Therefore, in his absence, there was quick swing in the tug-of-war in the opposite direction. To be clear, this did not cause all to feel the same degree of belonging as they had felt prior to this leadership, but this did cause a quick and dramatic shift in congregational identity of the church.

A member who had left during this period stated, "[We returned] the first Sunday that [he left], which probably wasn't very kind now that I look back, but the first Sunday we knew because we had good friends. We were in communication with [friends] who were still a part of the community. We came home." This member's own subgroup identity as a woman who wished to lead was very salient, and the emphasis of the contrasting congregational identity caused very little belonging for her at the church in the above left chart. The absence of the pastor allowed the sense of belonging to RAC to be much stronger through the reduction of differentiation and the movement towards neutral within the contrasting congregational identity (figure 10).

The Alliance Canada and Women in Ministry

The women interviewed at Riverdale Alliance did not feel supported through the leadership of Riverdale during these years, and they felt that concerns which were brought up with denominational leadership were met with a lack of concern and an inadequate response. Furthermore, it was felt by some that the denominational leadership did not provide the

---

either joined a new community temporarily or did not attend any church and informed their friends of the reasons behind this. Thus, the intentionality of these members to leave presents an interesting juxtaposition in their sense of still belonging to the community despite formally withdrawing.

appropriate accountability for the leadership. On top of these issues, The Alliance Canada has, both in the history of Riverdale Alliance and nationally, presented inconsistent guidelines to churches on the role of women in Christian leadership. During my presentation to John, he said (sarcastically), "Surely the lack of a clear and definite position with frameworks and guidelines helped immensely! To let the misogynists know they don't have a place." The Christian and Missionary Alliance in Canada (C&MA, also known as The Alliance Canada) has a complex history with women ministers. Founded by A.B. Simpson in the early twentieth century, the organization initially saw itself as a missional and evangelistic association rather than a church. Women church planters led ministries like men, but their ministry role remained unchanged. In 1928, women were renamed deaconesses instead of elders, but their ministry role remained unchanged. In 1960, the C&MA president declared the organization a church denomination, making women leadership emphasized. Opponents of women in church leadership either supported or disagreed with it. When the Canadian C&MA became autonomous (functioning separately from the US denomination), a new form of governance was found, where a church did not have an executive board but only had elders. This presented difficulties in defining elders and impacted women who had been functionally serving in such roles. In 1988, a motion was passed that suggested that in the biblical pattern and historical practice of The Christian and Missionary Alliance, elders in the church have usually been men. However, a new president in 1992 argued this was incorrect. In 1996, a woman was nominated for a denominational board of directors, leading to emotional debate. In 1998, a motion was passed to not restrict women from national- or district-level boards of directors or from administering ordinances. In 2000, the board of directors stated that Alliance Christians with a high view of Scripture have been unable to arrive at a consensus on whether women can serve on the board of elders. Following a debate, churches were allowed by a 2/3 majority vote to allow women to serve on the board of elders. While there was no precedent for women being called elders, there was precedent for women serving in leadership capacities, which became known as eldership in 1981. In 2008, a new licensing policy was enacted without language restricting roles to men. In 2016, and 2022, a statement affirming the equal, gifted, and empowered role of men and women in ministry affirms their role in biblical leadership and global mandate while allowing local churches to choose complementarian or egalitarian stances.[7]

Processing the Pain

After the resignation of the aforementioned pastor, a transitional pastor was hired. During this time, there was much grieving and processing. According to one member, there were leaders in the church who had very strong, "legalistic" views. One belief that was brought up was a strong complementarian stance, which was not shared by all members of the community. While one member found alignment with the church's identity, they held more egalitarian views on gender roles than the church officially held. Despite this difference, she chose to moderate her views, seeking to maintain peace within the church. Internally, however, she longed for a more inclusive approach that would allow for broader participation and involvement. Another participant found belonging within the church's commitment to complementarianism and suggested that change in this area would impact his sense of belonging within the church. Another member acknowledged personal growth and exploration in certain areas compared to the church's identity, such as sexual identity and gender roles, and also recognized the value and importance of the church's identity. For this person, it was about striking a balance between personal growth and embracing the collective identity of the church community.

Program Changes

During the time of the recent transitional pastor, there was also a rapid reduction in the programs that were run. This was exacerbated by the COVID-19 pandemic, where all of the programs run by churches had to be cancelled or significantly altered. One member stated that the transitional pastor "did a great job of leading us through a lot of the problems. He didn't

---

7. In the interest of reflexivity, it is important for me to acknowledge that the issue of confusion on this issue has impacted family and colleagues of mine. Alliance women colleagues have expressed frustration and awkwardness in being licensed but struggling to find churches that accept them in leadership positions. Furthermore, there is no clarity, to my knowledge, of the ability of a woman to be elected to denominational leadership such as district superintendent or president. This creates situations where, as an attempt to accommodate complementarian workers, female workers who were licensed, ordained, and given freedom to speak are excluded from preaching in certain capacities.

get it all done, he left a few things for [the new pastor] to take care of. But he got a long way." Out of this, there was a decision to focus on discipleship. A significant theme for the church was the book *Simple Church: Returning to God's Process for Making Disciples*. Out of this book came the process of reducing the programming done by the church and focusing on a few simple aspects. There was also a particular focus on small groups. One member stated, "The small groups are important because small groups are where you build community. You get to know one another, and you share each other's burdens. You participate in family life, and you learn more about the gospel. And so it's there to help you sort of deepen your faith." In the survey results, the second-highest gathering which members felt they were an integral part of the community was small groups. This was extremely high among Millennial respondents and a high majority of all other generations responded similarly, suggesting an overall attraction towards small groups. An interesting result was found in the low importance assigned by the War Kids generation towards church dinners, ministry teams, and informal meetings with church members. The lack of the role in ministry teams may have been due to elderly members of the church not holding formal roles, but the low numbers towards ministry teams and informal meetings was somewhat surprising. This was surprising to Pastor John as well, as he stated, "I wonder why War Kids are not for church dinners and informal meetings." John suggested that there may have been confusion around the wording that may have affected the responses. During the interviews, there were not any narrative trends which provided any insight on why these trends may exist. While it does not seem to be a significant area of concern for Riverdale, it remains an interesting piece of data which may uncover more aspects of the communal identity at some point, as church leaders reflect on this data.

 The process of simplifying church programs also caused issues among members, who felt that losing the former programs meant losing elements of what the church was. One member said, "It's a very difficult thing for some people to let go of what we always did. And we always did the same thing every year. And we're wanting to get away from that and letting go of women's ministries and men's ministries and whatever we did, you know, children's programs and so on. It's hard." Another member who said they were "not a fan" of simple church described it as follows:

> They encourage you to put everything into the small group and that includes your potluck suppers and your entertainment and

all of that. And as a result, you get to know your small group well, but you don't have the same opportunities of getting to know other people because we don't have a women's group. My observation is that it narrows the church because you're stuck in your small group.

Many of the people interviewed spoke favorably of the small groups, saying it was where "deeper community" was felt. Other members felt that it was a way for newcomers to connect relationally within a church. It has been my observation that perceiver readiness is a key factor in the salient differentiation which occurred in some members. For example, one interviewee identified strongly with the subgroup formed through a women's group, and so the dissolution of that subgroup identity into this new congregational identity caused her own personal practices and traits to become differentiated. However, for others, there was not a perceived readiness to see the simple church identity as differentiated from their own, and thus the change did not significantly affect their belonging. With figure 11 we can visualize how the change away from a programmatic church towards the simple church model affected (non)belonging in RAC. [8]

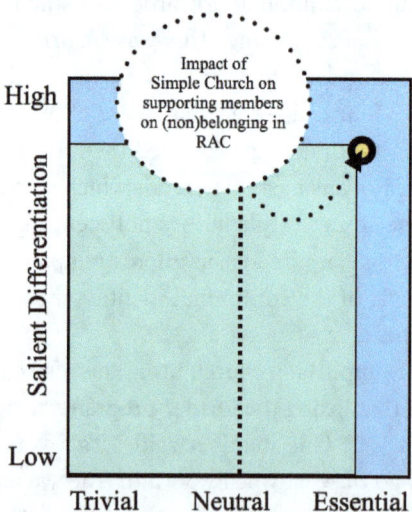

Figure 11: TEST: Simple Church in RAC

8. While figure 11 looks at the belonging supporting members, the converse subgroup will have a similar chart showing non-belonging. This is due to alignment of the beliefs and practices of supporting members' and converse non-alignment of non-supporting members' beliefs and practice with their perceived stereotype of the wider group of RAC.

The focus of the previous and current pastor on the "simple church" model through teaching and programming changes continued to cause the chosen congregational identity of being a "simple church" to move through emphasis towards becoming an essential identity. For the majority subgroup, this did not cause significant differentiation, but for a small subgroup, there was high salience in this area. The result of this is a high level of non-belonging in those who do not support the simple church model.

The responses regarding the alignment between individuals' own identities and the perceived collective identities of RAC vary. Some individuals feel a strong alignment and share the church's vision and values, while others may have differing views or areas of disagreement but still find common ground and value in their involvement with the church. Some participants align closely with the church's beliefs and mission, finding their own passions and values reflected in the church's identity. Others may hold different perspectives on specific issues, such as gender roles or social engagement, but choose to moderate their views for the sake of maintaining harmony within the church community. Overall, there is a recognition that personal identity and church identity can evolve and grow together, with individuals finding both alignment and freedom to explore and shape their own beliefs within the context of the church's broader identity.

Sense of Belonging

Overall, the survey responses reflect a strong identification with church community and a high sense of belonging. Among the interview participants, the majority expressed a strong sense of belonging within their church community. Nearly all participants at some point felt a strong sense of belonging within their respective church communities, finding connection, support, and a place to grow in their faith. However, a few participants did mention feeling like outsiders at certain points. Julia experienced moments of feeling like an outsider when cliques formed within the church community, while Jean felt like an outsider during a period of spiritual abuse and when their voice was not heard.

Identity Tug of War

Identity Scale Compared to Riverdale Average

	Riverdale	Average Riverdale
Female	4.08	
Male		4.29
Millenials	3.92	
Gen X		4.3
Boomers	4.11	
War Kids	4.12	

3   5

Figure 12: Survey Results: RAC: Identity Scale: Comparative Summary

When the church leadership dismissed their concerns, James and Megan also felt like outsiders. Overall, while most participants felt a strong sense of belonging, there were instances where some individuals felt excluded or unheard within the church community. The responses regarding feeling like an outsider in the church varied among the participants. Julia mentioned improvements in the inclusion of women, while John expressed a disconnect with churches focused on programs rather than personal transformation. Lydia shared experiences of being ostracized in the past, while Danielle did not feel like an outsider despite being divorced. Violet expressed concern about changes in the church and competition with another church. Megan mentioned feeling isolated due to communication and administrative barriers, while James emphasized the importance of fellowship beyond the church building. Overall, the participants had mixed experiences, with some feeling connected and accepted, while others occasionally experienced feelings of isolation or disconnection.

Openness to Outsiders

According to participants, RAC is generally open and welcoming to outsiders and newcomers, with members actively reaching out and creating an inclusive atmosphere. However, there are variations in the level of openness and engagement, depending on individuals and their awareness of the church's past emotional wounds. Some participants expressed the church's desire to improve its embrace of diversity, including the LGBTQ community and individuals from different backgrounds. During the presentation, John reflected on this, saying, "I chuckle because some of these people have no idea that we have someone who is connected that is married to someone of the same sex. . . . Like people want us to be more welcome to the LGBTQ [community], Okay, well how do I say we are without outing literally the individual that is connected, right?" This response may represent recognizing that salient differentiation occurs for the LGBTQ members of the church. In fact, Pastor John may be indicating a fear of creating salience, even through a emphasis on inclusion, due to the current low salience that this member experiences. While the exact reasons for this response are not known, this highlights how complex this issue is to Pastor John. Overall, the church aims to be open and welcoming, recognizing the importance of bringing in new people and creating connections beyond initial greetings. The church has made strides in becoming more diverse and open, with a better mix of people from different backgrounds. RAC recognizes the barriers that may hinder outsiders from fully engaging with the church community. Participants in the interviews provided suggestions on how to lower these barriers. It should be noted that these suggestions do not necessarily reflect agreement or disagreement on the part of the researcher; rather, they are a report of suggestions from interviewees. The participants emphasized the importance of creating a more welcoming environment for the LGBTQ community and individuals of diverse backgrounds. Adapting church activities and services to be relatable and appealing to people in today's society was also highlighted. Deepening connections and fostering fellowship among members were seen as key to making newcomers feel a sense of belonging. It was suggested to reevaluate statements and policies that may act as barriers and focus on accepting individuals without judgment. Establishing a youth ministry, increasing the church's visibility through community events, and providing support for new visitors were additional strategies mentioned.

The participants reflected on what it means for RAC to be a welcoming community. According to John, it involves inviting people into a transformative relationship with God and fostering spiritual growth. Jacob emphasized the importance of friendliness, service, and helping newcomers connect. Danielle emphasized care and making individuals feel valued. George saw a welcoming community as one that welcomes strangers without judgment and guides them through the process of becoming members. Jean valued a safe and accepting environment for people with challenges or unconventional backgrounds. James highlighted the significance of friendly greetings and genuine involvement. Lydia emphasized the need for fellowship and openness to change. Megan acknowledged the church's efforts but suggests further improvements, including spaces for young people and a focus on discipleship. Overall, a welcoming community at RAC involves genuine care, inclusivity, spiritual growth, and a willingness to adapt and embrace change. Generally speaking, there was a sense that there has been an overall reduction of differentiation and a movement towards being more welcoming. This could be seen potentially as a reduction in the polarization between female and male members. This reduction represents a trivialization of particular traits which causes a decrease in differentiation.

RAC's congregational identity encompasses several key aspects. The church places a strong emphasis on service, actively engaging in various social programs and initiatives to support the marginalized and those in need. There are specific requirements for ministry involvement, including a period of observation, membership, and adherence to the church's statement of faith and policies. Creating a welcoming environment and helping individuals find their place within the community are priorities, along with fostering simplicity, discipleship, and spiritual growth. Unconditional love and acceptance are valued, encouraging support for individuals facing internal battles. The church promotes a sense of community and belonging, emphasizing active engagement, small group participation, and discipleship.

Summary

RAC has undergone significant transformations, navigated challenges, and sought healing from past spiritual traumas. Despite these obstacles, there is a shared commitment to being a welcoming and inclusive community. The participants highlight the importance of love, acceptance, and fellowship within the church, as well as the need for ongoing growth and adaptation. RAC is characterized by a desire to reach out to newcomers, create connections, and foster spiritual growth. Their congregational identity is shaped by commitment to discipleship, simplicity, and service to others. These conversations reveal a community that is resilient in the midst of challenges, seeking to align its congregational identity with God's vision, and striving to create an environment where all individuals can feel a sense of belonging and grow in their faith. RAC's collective identity is characterized by a journey of healing and recovery from past spiritual traumas. The church strives to be friendly and welcoming to all who enter its doors, despite grappling with confusion and transition in its programs and ministry approaches. It places importance on hospitality, worship, and love within the church community. RAC has faced immense turbulence, including leadership changes, cliques, abusive leadership, toxic splits, attendance fluctuations, and high pastoral turnover, not to mention challenges due to the pandemic and Canadian culture. While the church is known internally for its harmonious and friendly atmosphere, it faces challenges in overcoming its past of division and conflict. The church is in a period of change, envisioning a future aligned with God's vision and bringing renewed life to its members. It prioritizes discipleship and endeavors to love, build, and equip believers while maintaining a simple and welcoming approach to gatherings and events.

KORADAI ALLIANCE CHURCH

Demographics

The survey respondents were made up of 53 percent male and 47 percent female, representing a fairly even split. The age range of respondents included 47 percent Baby Boomers, 33 percent Gen X, and 20 percent Millennial and Gen Z. The interviews were conducted with three male members of the church community. All of the interviewees have begun to attend within the past two years, with one individual having attended the church in the past prior to an extended break. The weaknesses of this sample size within interviews are a lack of diversity in gender and a lack of representation of longer-term members of the church community. Given those weaknesses, there will likely be gaps within these narratives and the history of the church. These gaps may hinder a comprehensive understanding of the church's development and dynamics over a longer period of time. Additionally, the absence of female perspectives limits the overall perspective on the church community and its experiences. This presents an important gap in the ability to access salient differentiation based on differences (both direct and indirect) due to factors surrounding gender. Including a more diverse range of interviewees would provide a more holistic portrayal of the church's history and its impact on its members. Furthermore, there is a blind spot in the narratives related to potential issues where gender is relevant. Nonetheless, the interviewees all provided helpful details for this narrative study. Their insights shed light on the church's growth, its role in the community, and the personal transformations experienced by its members. Despite the limitations, their stories contribute to a comprehensive understanding of the church's history and its significance in shaping individuals' lives. Furthermore, it should be noted that the goal of this narrative study is not to provide a historical study, but to identify existing narratives from a variety of perspectives and examine the effectiveness of this methodology. By examining the various perspectives on the church's collective identity, role in the community, and personal transformations, these insights offer valuable perspectives on how the church's identity has evolved into its existing form.

Story of KAC

Formation / Early Years

There was not significant information gained regarding the initial formation of Koradai Alliance Church. Most of the history shared did not go back to the foundations. However, there were some details shared. These details included the approximate time period when Koradai Alliance Church was established and some key events in the church history. Additionally, some insights were provided about the early leaders or key figures who played a role in shaping the church's early development. However, a comprehensive understanding of the church's initial formation and its early challenges still remains elusive due to the limited amount of information shared.

The church was started roughly forty years ago. Around thirty years ago, the current church meeting space was built. There is a group of about six to eight current members who were part of the founding members of the church. One interviewee saw this as "a good thing." The founding members have seen a lot of change in the church, but according to one participant, they seem to agree with the basic tenants of where the church is. They believe that the church has remained true to its essential values and mission, despite the challenges it has faced over the years. These founding members were also asked to stand up and speak by the new pastor during a recent celebratory setting. This was seen, according to one source, as an act of respect towards the history of the church.

Previous Pastor

Prior to the current pastor, there was a transitional time which was preceded by a pastor who was at KAC for about seven to eight years. There was little shared about the history before this pastor, except that there was a high level of turnover in pastors and employees. According to one source,

> They went through employees quite quickly. They were welcomed in the front door and booted out the back . . . and there was a lot of hurt—obviously with the ones that were fired, but also musicians. There was a bunch of them. . . . There's quite a few that never got back on their feet and have never gone back to any kind of a church setting since that day.

The aforementioned pastor came during a time where there was a lot of division in the congregation. Few details were shared or known about these divisions. The previous pastor felt that the church was united and his task of reuniting and focusing was completed, which was the reason he gave for leaving. This surprised and confused some members, with one interviewee stating,

> There was definitely some tensions somewhere along the way that I can glean, but I don't know any of the details. And then the previous pastor was able to work through most of those problems, and I will call it reuniting or focusing the congregation. And then once that task, if you will, was completed, as far as he was concerned, he decided it was time for him to move on to another church, which I found interesting and surprising. He came in during a time where there was a lot of division amongst the congregants. I don't know any of the details of that, but I mean, typical church stuff. I guess for many churches there's always conflicts. I wouldn't say necessarily it was a united church at that point in time, just because of COVID and how everybody has different views, different opinions on many things surrounding COVID. But people were willing to put those aside sort of thing and come together as a congregation kind of thing.

It is clear that the normative fit of a unified church for this member was different than the pastor. Furthermore, there may have been a differences of perception to the trivialization of salient differentiation. This pastor may have found from his perspective that the church was unified, yet this member saw growing differentiation. The previous pastor also had a significantly different personality than the current pastor. One interviewee said, "He used to come into his office and as soon as it was time for the service to start, he walked in, sat in his seat, did what he had to do, and if they had a meeting, he sat in the meeting, and as soon as it was finished, he got up and left. There was no communication and fellowship." This was not something which seemed to be an issue with church leadership, which was surprising for the current pastor.

Current Pastor

After the resignation of this pastor, there was a transition process with an interim pastor. Little was shared around the details of this time except that there were many different visiting preachers during this season. The current pastor of Koradai, Michael, started approximately six months prior to the interviews taking place. Michael's previous ministry was at a very different culture on a different continent. He has expressed that this season has been filled with excitement as well as anxiety. He says that the anxiety is about experiencing God differently in Canada than other places: "I find a very different version of God and His church in Canada, which is one of the struggles I'm grappling with at the moment." According to one member, one of the focuses of Pastor Michael has been to try to reach out and get ahold of people hurt by the church to try to bring healing to pain. Michael's perspective as someone outside of Canadian society caused the differentiation from being a cross-cultural minister to grow in salience. This both had a positive effect on his self-awareness of the church and a negative effect on the simplicity of leading ministry. However, Michael overall saw this as a net positive, as this removed blind spots which other Canadian pastors might not be aware of.

Several people described Koradai Alliance Church as "middle of the road" and "not too legalistic." For these individuals, their perceived readiness of what it looks like for a church to be on a polarized extreme caused this aspect of KAC to be more emphasized. The addition of a new pastor was described as transforming the congregation's identity in many ways. Sources also spoke positively of the casual dress which can be worn without judgement, again tying to a salient readiness based on previous affiliation of churches where this was not the case. For those members who never experienced formal dress in a church setting, this subgroup identity would likely be much less salient, even if important. The backgrounds of the members were described to be a wide variety of denominational ties, which creates a wide variety in the style of personal worship during services. Some are very charismatic in their worship, and others are very reserved. On Koradai's lower denominational affiliation than average respondents, Michael felt this made sense due to the number of different denominational backgrounds represented. He described this reality as something which he was pleased about, but found it difficult to lead at the moment. This reflects a situation where there is an increase in the salient differentiation between intragroup church identities based on comparative fit of denominational background differences. The congregants who were used to being surrounded by a certain "type" of Christian became aware of differences in ways that would not have been salient before. However, there is also a clear push towards trivialization of that differentiation.

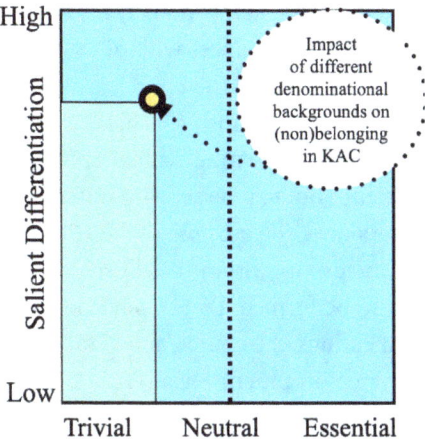

Figure 13: TEST: Different Denominational Backgrounds in KAC

In addition, through these divisions, there likely emerged a high degree of perceiver readiness to see these differences—i.e., "What does this church teach on x," or "Does this church do y?" As this differentiation increases, it has the potential to begin to push people out of belonging. However, due to Michael's efforts to trivialize the salient different identities of different denominational backgrounds, the degree of belonging has stayed relatively consistent. This has been done in a number of ways, including welcoming different perspectives, welcoming the diversity of worship styles, and addressing these differences. Michael reported that, through his leadership, he hopes to drive away some of the contextual polarizing difference with a shared stronger congregational identity towards mission.

Shared Identity of Koradai

Tent Meetings

Every person interviewed highlighted summer tent meetings as a significant event in the church's recent history. These were a way to reach out into the community and bring people together. The tent meetings provided an opportunity for individuals to connect with one another, share their faith, and foster a sense of unity within the church family. Will mentioned the church's tent meetings held in August, specifically aimed at engaging with the community. During these meetings, attendees were encouraged not to sit exclusively with friends but to interact with unfamiliar individuals, especially those who came alone. The purpose of these interactions was to foster a sense of unity and inclusivity within the church and create opportunities for new connections to be formed. By actively engaging with the community during the tent meetings, the church aimed to break down barriers and promote a welcoming environment for all. Additionally, these gatherings provided a platform for individuals to share their personal experiences and testimonies, further strengthening the sense of faith and unity within the community.

These tent meetings and barbecues served as crucial opportunities for the church to connect with people who are not typically part of the congregation. Members of the community who heard about the church's events attended these gatherings out of curiosity. Through the interviews, it seemed that this was a significant shift in the narrative of the church. This provides an interesting other side of the previous scale. While the scale (figure 13) was, in the previous use, shown to demonstrate that denominational differences were made more trivial through a developed congregational identity of shared mission across denominational differences, this example shows in effect "the other side of the coin." As the differentiation—not only with other denominations, but also with the community in general—shifted away from essential with these unifying events, the result was a movement of shared mission towards essential.

This outreach effort helped bridge the gap between the church and the wider community. They were able to engage in conversations and activities that helped break down barriers and build relationships. Often times, these events are thought to break down barriers to "outsiders" of the church with entering the church, but the nature of this event also had a different effect. It appears that the degree of differentiation between the subgroups which fall within the church and outside the church were decreased, thus lowering a barrier to belonging both from the church community to those outside, and vice versa. The church saw these events to extend their outreach and make a positive impact on the wider community, but they also helped to shift the church's perspective towards a congregational identity which includes their surrounding community.

Shared Identity of Members

In reflecting on what makes them feel especially part of the Koradai Alliance community, the interview participants highlighted various aspects and events. Joel pointed out the recent tent meetings and barbecues, which attracted new faces from the local community and served as a starting point for outreach. Michael emphasized the significance of Sunday morning services, considering them a central and unifying element of the church community. He also highlighted the Wednesday night prayer meetings he initiated, which grew in attendance over time, fostering a sense of connection among attendees who came to pray, share, and support one another in their faith journey. Will discussed his involvement in an outreach group ministering to migrant workers, particularly those from Jamaica and Mexico. This group offers support through prayer, provides Bibles to those who need them, and even brings some of the workers to Sunday services at Koradai Alliance. This outreach effort allowed Will to feel deeply connected to the church community while serving others.

Interview participants felt that their personal identity aligns mostly well with the identity of KAC, but there are a few areas where they see divergence. One person came from a unique church background where everyone with a role in the church preached and described a difference due to perceived readiness in a church which has pastor-driven leadership. Another person identified an appreciation for the communal attitude of the church, including a willingness to clean up after lessons. For this person, the comparative fit between KAC and their previous church made this aspect obvious. Michael identified a few areas where he struggles, not just specifically with KAC, but with similar churches in general. He expressed frustration with feeling that the church seems to be run by bylaws and procedures which supersede God's word. He also shared past experiences of being frustrated with people who are unwilling to make a decision.

Identity Scale Compared to Koradai Average

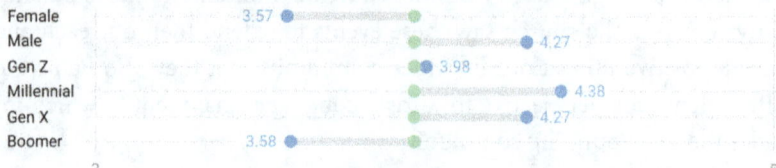

Identity Scale Compared to Total Average

Figure 14: Survey Results: KAC: Identity Scale

Reducing Barriers

Reducing Barriers Within the Church

Michael pointed out a few barriers he observed in the church, such as the prioritization of nuclear families over the biblical family, the lack of a sacrificial mindset, and the adoption of worldly ideologies within the church. He expressed concern about the reluctance to challenge "sacred cows" and emphasized the importance of using one's gifts within the church family rather than volunteering. Michael noted the challenge of introducing change into an established church with a different approach and the resistance it can generate. Will mentioned that the only significant barrier to belonging for him in the church context is requirements around church membership, and his personal conviction against it has prevented him from taking on certain roles within the church.

> I've been convicted not to become a member of anything.... There are others who feel the same way, but we're clearly in the minority. ... [A] couple of weeks ago, I was asked to be on a pastoral team, which is pretty self-explanatory. However, we were told weeks ago that I couldn't do that unless I became a member. So, I said, "Okay, I'll step aside." It's not a problem for us in that sense. But it did leave a bit of a sour taste because I didn't expect that requirement.

> Maybe I could understand it for the elder role, but for a pastoral role, which is a bit lower profile and not an elected position, it still came up. So, it was a little disappointing when you think you're in the right spot and then they throw you a curveball like that.

For Will, there is a difference of beliefs which became salient on this issue. He sees himself aligned on most issues, but when the issue of membership comes up, the differentiation between his views and the church's policy become salient. Thus, when this particular issue is discussed, his differences become very salient; but in most cases, they do not. Joel could not identify specific barriers to belonging at the moment but acknowledged the potential for improvements in various ministries and better organization. He also mentioned that the church is going through a period of change and redefinition of roles under new leadership.

In reflecting on whether it is more important for a church to be close-knit or open to outsiders, the perspectives varied among the sources. Will emphasized the significance of being open to outsiders, highlighting the shift from churches deeply rooted in generations of families to a more inclusive approach. He emphasized that people attend their church not out of familial obligation but because they feel it is where they fit in. On the other hand, Joel's perspective landed in the middle, acknowledging the value of being open while underscoring the importance of a close-knit community within the church. Michael brought a unique perspective by addressing the need to de-jargonize Christian language and challenge non-biblical concepts adopted by the church, such as the clergy-laity distinction and the separation between Sunday events and daily life. He critiqued the historical transformation of the church from a fellowship centered on the living Christ to an institutionalized enterprise. Michael also touched on the impact of colonialism in Africa, which disrupted traditional ways of living with the land. An example was provided of how indigenous African tribes once practiced rotational land use, allowing the earth to heal itself, a concept that contrasted starkly with the exploitative practices of colonial powers.

Michael's commitment to breaking down barriers and promoting a sense of community among different denominations was seen in a positive light to those who were interviewed. This collaborative approach has not only strengthened church relationships but also fostered a spirit of cooperation in serving the local community. Joel spoke about the wide variety of backgrounds within the church.

> I mean, we have all kinds of people from all walks of life and we have, every now and again, one of these people will stand up and give part of their life story sort of thing. And I just sort of sit there and I'm just stunned at what happened to them. And it's just like, wow. And they're of course looking for people like them to also integrate into the church.

Joel also emphasized that the pastor's commitment to breaking down barriers has led to a more welcoming environment within the church. He stated that the pastor's efforts have inspired other local churches to take a similar collaborative approach, further strengthening the community's overall sense of unity. He emphasized the significance of community outreach in engaging locals and potentially attracting them to the church. For Joel, the pastor's unique cultural background provides him with a unique perceiver readiness for identifying biases, challenging traditions, breaking down barriers, and fostering belonging. Will shared about the diversity of those at the church as well, saying,

> I find that our local church is very open because you've got very committed believers, lifelong newbies; they're all over the map. Some don't speak English too well. So, everyone's welcome there, and no one feels second-rate. Nobody feels second-rate for any other reason that I can ever see; not wealth or poverty either, really. Sometimes I bring in some homeless people in the morning, and lots of people welcome them. They sometimes sit a little closely, they do smell a little different, but everyone's still, "Hey, how are you? My name's so and so." So, I'm very proud of our tribe in that way. They do welcome people.

Michael highlighted a sense of cautious optimism within the church about its direction. The church's growth has brought both unifying and dividing factors. He acknowledged that the church's growth has brought about a greater sense of unity among its members, as they come from diverse backgrounds and experiences. However, he also recognized that this growth has led to some differences in opinions and perspectives within the congregation, which they are actively working to address and navigate together. Speaking specifically on the ages of those involved, he said,

> We have the privilege of having about half a dozen through a dozen of our founding members still in the church. And they constantly get acknowledgments from me if there's like, if we have baptism candidates and we issue out a certificate, I call them to come and

hand out the certificate.... So there's a constant participation from across the age variance in our church. Even in our prayer time, we get youngsters to come and pray and older folk and in between.

Outreach initiatives have engaged immigrant workers in particular, leading to their attendance, with Spanish interpretations provided during services. This approach has, at times, sparked discomfort among some church members who find it disruptive. Michael acknowledged that church growth comes with challenges, especially as new people join, and he joked, "I love the church. It's people I can't stand." These perspectives show a movement of the church towards both an increase in salient differentiation for subgroups of Spanish and non-Spanish speakers, but also a strong trivializing of language and ethnicity as not essential to the shared congregational identity of the church. Similarly to the aforementioned chart, the below chart represents the movement which Michael has encouraged in the church. Note that Michael, in this setting, cannot change the contextual identity of being different from one another, but the movement which he effects as a leader involves shifting perceiver readiness, and it has the potential to shift these salient subgroup identities and hence to reduce their impact on (non-)belonging.[9] The result of this shift means that there is, for Koradai, a higher salient awareness of internal differences, yet this has not (for most members) impeded their sense of belonging at Koradai.

---

9. The nature of the "mission" which Michael feels they are united with is certainly a major factor here. Michael expressed a mission which included working in unity across denominational lines and being a church who serves the community. Other "missions" may have quite the opposite effect, such as a mission which reflects a divisive or polarizing position against other churches and wider society. However, it is also not just this viewpoint that has caused the movement here; rather, it is the coupling of that view of mission with the shared sense of mission among congregants. In other words, a pastor could have the same view as Michael and see no shift due to a lack of the church sharing this sense of mission, and similarly, a church could have a strong sense of mission but with a very different perspective than Michael, causing dramatically different effects.

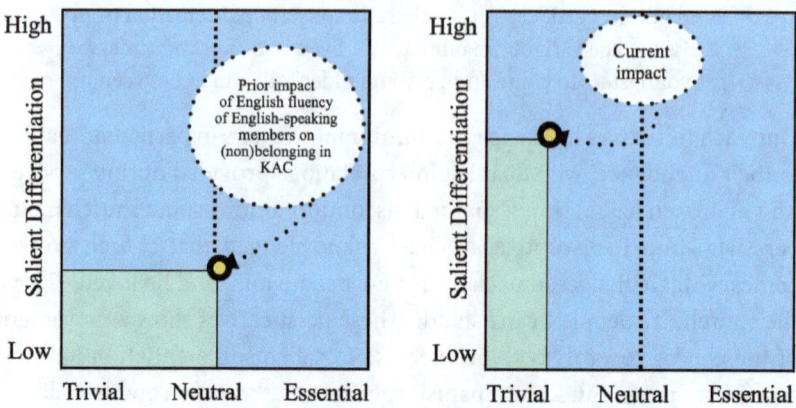

Figure 15: TEST: English Speakers in KAC

One aspect that is interesting about this case is that the actual degree of belonging has not shifted here, but the differentiation has increased. In such an environment, a sense of shared identity amongst those who are different can be fostered, deepening community. This would be done through the trivialization of intragroup identities that might otherwise foster division. This does not mean these identities are non-existent or even unimportant for individuals, but there is a movement to see English fluency as not essential to being a part of the church.

The church has faced challenges in welcoming newcomers, particularly those from different socioeconomic backgrounds. Historically, the church had been in a middle-class and affluent setting, which posed some hurdles in creating a warmly welcoming environment for diverse individuals. In response, Michael and his wife have taken personal initiative by greeting people at the church's entrance and even offering newcomers the opportunity for one-on-one conversations over coffee in the pastor's office. He also mentioned the formation of a pastoral team aimed at improving the church's approach to newcomers.

When considering what it means for Koradai Alliance Church to be a welcoming community, one source praised the church's welcoming attitude towards visitors and emphasized its inclusivity regardless of one's background or appearance. They recounted instances of bringing in individuals who may not conform to societal norms and noted how they were warmly received within the church. Joel similarly noticed significant changes in the church's approach to outreach over the past year:

> A year ago, I would've said [KAC] was closed [to outsiders] because there were no outreach programs per se. But in a year's time, that has completely changed. Now, we have outreach ministries to the immigrant workers, and that has brought in at least five or six gentlemen from outside the country who are here on work permits. The pastor has also organized tent meetings this summer and invited anyone from around the area. We've sent out flyers and done as much promotion as we can. The new pastor has even contacted all the churches in the city, which I found surprising because he wants to organize the entire city together. It's interesting. The word has been spread: "New pastor, new ideas, come take a look." From the inside out, it looks more friendly and open, but I'm not on the outside, so I don't know.

Another source also appreciated the church's commitment to fostering a sense of community, even during events like tent meetings, where the congregation actively sought to connect with newcomers in a genuine and organic manner. Another member acknowledged the complexity of the question and highlighted the diversity within the church, with people from various walks of life sharing their life stories. They recognized the wealth of worldly experiences among church members, providing a unique opportunity to connect with newcomers facing similar challenges. They believed that the church possessed powerful testimonies that could resonate with others and emphasized the importance of reaching out to people who might benefit from these connections and shared experiences.

Reducing Barriers Between Churches

Michael narrated his proactive approach to fostering connections with other pastors in the area. He recounted a specific incident when a member from another church began attending Koradai Alliance. In response, Michael reached out to the pastor of that church, not only to discuss the presence of the individual but also to initiate a culture of open communication and collaboration among local churches. He shared another anecdote involving a situation where a man from a different church was seeking assistance in finding a children's worker. In this context, Michael stressed the significance of maintaining lines of communication between churches and expressed his disappointment when pastors approached his church without prior consultation. He underscored the importance of trust and cooperation within the broader Christian community while recounting these experiences.

Others who were interviewed identified that Michael has actively sought out other churches in the city in order to foster a collaborative approach, finding this "surprising." Michael seeks to reduce the strong comparative differentiation which occurs out of denominational divides in this community. Michael's unique perceiver readiness due to his background has aided in identifying and addressing biases and traditions that may impede inclusivity. The church's collaborative approach has resulted in fruitful partnerships and joint initiatives with other churches in the community. Pastor Michael's actions shifted the church away from a congregational identity of focusing on internal growth and instead towards actively engaging with the needs of the community. This shift in prioritizing collaboration and community impact has caused the idealized identity of church independence, which was expressed to have been developed as essential in the past, to move towards trivial, and as this happens, the identity of interchurch unity increases.

Koradai has also been able to foster a more welcoming environment where people from diverse backgrounds feel welcome and valued by leveraging their unique perspective. There is a focus on inviting people who are not normally part of the church community and making the necessary changes to make the environment more welcoming, trivializing subgroup traits and practices that might otherwise produce salient differentiation and thus reduce experiences of belonging.

Reducing Barriers in Culture

Michael emphasized his belief that the church should exist to serve the community rather than expecting the community to serve the church. He also shared his reservations about the term "volunteerism," highlighting his preference for individuals to utilize their God-given gifts rather than simply making themselves available for tasks. Regarding the role of the church in a polarized culture, Michael advocated for a "both-and" approach rather than an "either-or" mindset, emphasizing coexistence and dialogue within the church. He proposed the concept of acceptance and the importance of loving neighbors, even when they hold different beliefs. In this way, Michael seeks to trivialize practices and traits which bring differentiation while emphasizing the identities of common humanity and being in the

Research Data

same community. The following graph represents the proposed reduction of polarizing beliefs, practices, and traits over the coming years. This particular TEST scale is unique in that it is something of a sweeping generalization, with the dots representing a collective of potential (and actual) polarizing beliefs, practices, and traits, collectively referred to as "polarizing aspects." These are understood to be the various beliefs, practices, and traits that Michael has in view when, as a leader, he contemplates his congregation and its social identity.

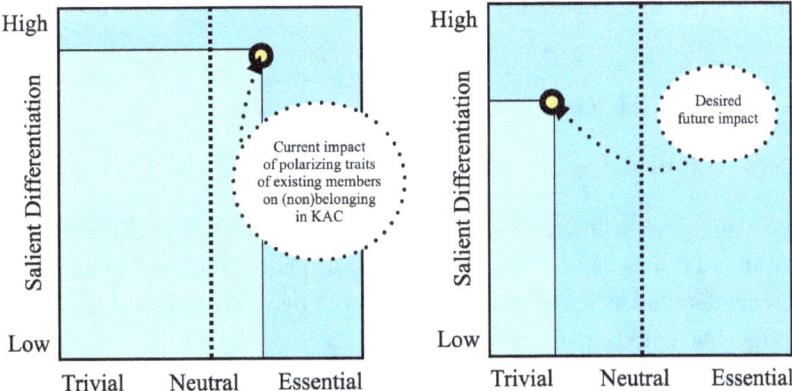

Figure 16: TEST: KAC in Koradai

Michael also discussed the post-COVID church, suggesting a need for fresh ideas and discussions on how to adapt to the changing landscape. He stressed the importance of reaching out to multicultural communities and strategically training young Christians as missionaries. Regarding the struggles faced by present-day leaders, Michael pointed out the competition with online platforms and the challenges of addressing diverse perspectives presented on platforms like YouTube. Michael also delved into the topic of distrust of institutions, mentioning a paper titled "Is Modern Missions Colonialism?" and reflecting on how mission movements historically led to the suppression of cultural practices. He raised the question of whether present-day missions should ask people to abandon their culture to follow Jesus or if they can come to Jesus with their culture intact.

Summary

The interview participants expressed hope that the discussion initiated by the research would encourage churches to reevaluate their role and importance in the community. They underscored the necessity of the local church as a place of belonging, guidance, and support, reminiscent of a time when people turned to the church as a source of wisdom and solutions in times of crisis. Recent changes from tent meetings, outreach to migrant workers, and shifts in leadership style have brought about a shift in the congregational identity of the church. Koradai Alliance Church is seeking to be a church which is both diverse and united. Pastor Michael is well aware of the difficulty of this task, but there is a sense of excitement in moving forward and ahead in a new way.

ARCHET CHURCH

Demographics

Archet Church is located in the suburban community of Archet, which is within an hour's drive to Toronto's downtown core. The demographics for Archet respondents represented an even split between male and female respondents, with 50 percent within each respective group. Nearly all respondents were either Gen X (50 percent) or Baby Boomers (40 percent) with a small portion being Gen Z (10 percent). There were no respondents from Archet from the Millennial or War Kids generation. This absence affects the survey results' ability to present data on these respective subgroups.

Story of Archet Church

Archet Church was formed approximately forty years ago, by a group of people "who believed that there ought to be an Alliance church here [in Archet]." They began meeting in a school, and the early history is described as fairly ordinary. However, around fifteen to twenty years ago, there was a church split formed over conflict around "charismatic" theological differences, and a group of approximately two hundred people left the church over issues with the charismatic elements of Archet church. One source believed that a reason for this shift came from a shift in the Alliance to return to its roots as a charismatic Holiness movement. This caused those who were used to a less charismatic worship service to protest against new elements within the congregation. However, the church was said to be now very healthy and positive, and in agreement with (current) denominational stances around charismatic theology. In this, there was a strong emphasis

RESEARCH DATA

towards a charismatic congregational identity. There was a willingness of church leaders to emphasize charismatic practices which became salient for the members of the church. The leadership was willing to cause a lack of comparative fit for individuals who had opposing views, and some individuals felt that they no longer belonged at Archet as a result. However, the majority of the church found an alignment in comparative fit with the salient identity of being a charismatic church. The following represents the charismatic identity of Archet as experienced by the current majority subgroup. In previous years, the charismatic identity became salient due to differentiated subgroups within the community, but there now is a low intragroup differentiation and therefore low salience as regards being a charismatic.

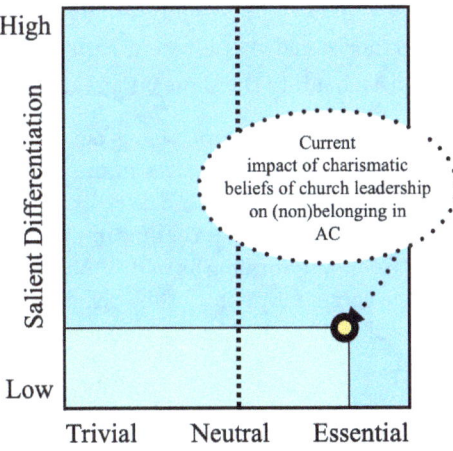

Figure 17: TEST: Charismatic Beliefs in Archet

Approximately fifteen years ago, Archet Church sold their church property, and with the funds, they would have been able to buy a large property outside of the town with a large building, but instead they chose to have a location which was downtown, present in the community of Archet. This decision was driven by their desire to remain accessible and connected to the local community. Opting for a downtown location, Archet Church aimed to be easily reachable for both their existing members and potential newcomers, fostering a stronger sense of community engagement. Additionally, being in downtown Archet allowed the church to actively participate in local events and initiatives, further strengthening their presence and impact within the town. As one interviewee put it, "We're in the heart of [Archet]." Given this focus, it is unsurprising that 70 percent of respondents lived ten km or under from the church's meeting space.

According to one interviewee, Archet's congregational identity is "rooted in the concept of presence." This principle guided their decision to move to a downtown location.

> Instead of buying a plot of land and building a nice big brand new building on the edge of town, they really were guided by the concept of presence and being the presence of God in the community, and believing that the presence of God and the spirit of God particularly dwells in the midst of its people in the church. And wherever they are, his presence is carried. And so the idea of moving into the culture hub of the city, into the downtown core of the city was all guided by this concept of presence.

This member also further stated that a recent shift towards personal discipleship ties back for Archet into the same congregational identity.

> And then recently the addition of seeing our primary invitation into discipleship is to put ourselves in the presence of God through different spiritual practices and disciplines and be formed by that. That is kind of the two sides of the same coin of presence, the presence of God for us forming us so that the presence of God through us to the community here, just by being active and present. So that would be like, the identity would be guided by that particular theme.

COVID was described as a very difficult time in the church's history, causing Archet Church to lose many members: "[During COVID] a lot of people that were part of Archet either moved away, moved for business, got tired of religion." Because of this, it felt like a church plant moving ahead. There was a redefining of the congregational identity of the church, and the result of this was a shift in the comparative fit between the congregants' stereotype of what the church had been and what the church was presently. Out of this, a freshness was described in this season as the church did not feel that they needed to continue what they always had done. The loss of members also presented an opportunity for Archet Church to redefine its focus and attract new individuals seeking spiritual fulfillment. This was done through an emphasis on various intergroup identities which correlate to the aforementioned vision. This shift allowed for a diverse and dynamic community to emerge, fostering a sense of growth and exploration within the church. The church has grown significantly, and with that growth, the average age of the attendee has decreased.

Identity Shifts from Growth

While there are many factors to which this recent growth can be attributed, one factor quickly shifted the dynamics of the church. A large church in Ontario was struggling significantly with the fallout from misconduct of a well-known pastor. This church had a very young demographic and was particularly attractive to those who found themselves uncomfortable in a traditional church environment. As a result, several sites of this church shut down, and the church's membership has dropped significantly. According to one source, Archet Church experienced a large influx of new families who left this large church. One interviewee expressed disappointment in some former members of Archet Church who had left due to the shift that came from the changing demographics of the church. The interviewee mentioned that the changing demographics of the church brought about a shift in its dynamics, with which some former members were not comfortable. This represented this group finding their normative fit between the congregational identity and their group identity becoming differentiated. According to this source,

> Now some people are leaving because they're like, "Too many young people, oh, all these families and I'm in my eighties, this is not comfortable for me anymore." So you're always gonna have, with a lead new leader and new growth, you're gonna have some transition. And I think that's where we're at. Not a lot, but just a few are like, "This isn't my, my small thirty group church anymore. This is now 180 and I'm not feeling comfortable anymore."

This reaction was seen to be the minority, and all who were interviewed expressed excitement around this growth. The recent shifts, both from the influx of members from another church and those who have not been part of a church, is an example of a reduction of intergroup identities which would promote segmenting "the church" and "the community." This results in a change of the perceived readiness between the church and "outsiders" due to the shift in stereotyping of those outside. As the growth of young families became more salient, this came along with an emphasis of a shared ideal identity as a church which is engaged missionally to be present in the downtown core. This brought an eventual sense of belonging to many, but for some, this also brought a deep sense of feeling like an outsider, resulting in their departure. As a church, they felt that the new direction caused by the newcomers justified the barrier to belonging to those who did not want to worship in this environment.

The church also seeks to engage with the downtown area they are located in and to be involved with the activities that happen on the street. Through the open atmosphere, they hope to foster an environment which is different than typical churches and focuses on walking relationally with one another and with God. One interview stated that in addition to being focused in their community,

> We're very focused on developing a deeper relationship with Christ. . . . That's what's being discussed on Sundays, preached on Sundays. So you really know what the church is focusing on. It's focusing on not just serving because we came from a church where all you did was serve and you didn't grow. This church is really focused on not growing intellectually, but growing your relationship deeper with Christ. And that's very, very strategic and very deliberate. That is not head smart. It's giving the tools of how you grow your relationship closer to Christ. Like practicing the Sabbath and doing prayer and learning about prayer and learning about Sabbath and learning about fasting for the purpose of having a deeper relationship with Christ.

By prioritizing relational connections and personal spiritual growth, the church aims to create a sense of community where individuals can authentically support and encourage one another in their spiritual journeys. Pastor Chris, who recently transitioned into the primary pastoral role, was pleased with the feeling that there was a continuity.

> The beautiful thing is it's been felt like there's a continuity of story and narrative and culture. The shift is in who's here to play it out or live or live it out. So that's one of the beautiful parts of this story. And a lot of transitions don't go like this. It feels like there's a real strong continuity between Pastor Steve and I and therefore [continuity with] the former elders and the new elders in vision, philosophy, and identity. So we haven't had to really convince people too much of that necessarily.

Research Data

Openness to Outsiders

The church was described by all interviewees as very open to newcomers. The atmosphere of the church was reflected with the open concept style of the building. The sudden growth has created a situation where about half of the congregation is very new to the church. One interviewee commented, "I'm sure in years to come we'll look back and say it was really chaotic, but it was also very welcoming, and we are hearing from people that they are coming back because they felt welcomed and felt that this could be a place of belonging for them." Another interviewee highlighted that the church is gifted at engaging with newcomers and inviting them into the community. This source believed the greeters are well-trained, and while admitting there is more they can always be doing, they believed the church was doing great job in welcoming people. They also described the need to not force an unnatural conversation, saying, "You have to take those cues, right? Some people wanna sit back and explore. But to those people who are open to conversations, it's very welcoming. Are we perfect? No. Do we miss people? Yeah." From the interviews, it appears that there has been an effort to emphasize being a welcoming church. The impression which they wish to leave on newcomers is one of correcting stereotypes which individuals have in the community about churches in general. In addition, they seek to emphasize practices and traits which would cause newcomers to experience low salience of the differentiation between themselves and the community. Conversely, they wish to identify and reduce or trivialize practices and traits which would make such differences salient.

While discussing whether it is a higher priority to be a close-knit community or be open to outsiders, there was a shared sense of a view that having close relationships is vital to being open to outsiders. It was suggested that the church should be "a close-knit community committed to being inviting to outsiders." All the interviewees highlighted the need to not have relationships that are exclusive to others, but also to foster a deep community that others can be invited into. When asked about what might foster that community, it was suggested that a shared agreement on vision and mission rather than theology is a driving force. In this, there would be a trivializing of theological differences and an emphasis on shared mission. As a result, belonging may initially suffer because a potential factor in self-categorization is trivialized. The overall salience of group identity within the church may be reduced as a result. However, leaders can emphasize shared mission as an important aspect of group identity. The shift in perceived readiness of individuals' alignment in a missional church can deepen a salient shared group identity within the church. Archet Church leadership showed a desire to shift theological difference towards being trivial and shifting a particular sense of mission towards being essential.

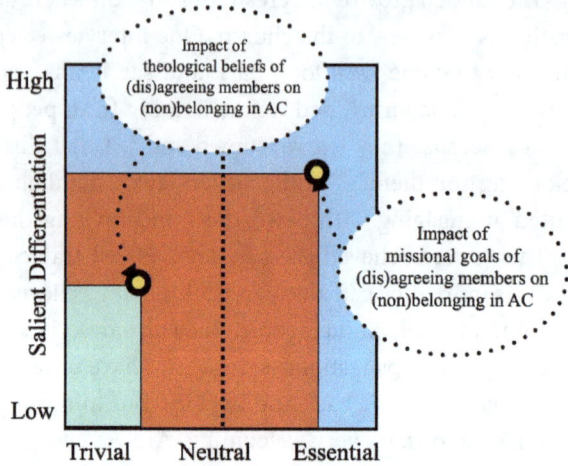

Figure 18: TEST Scale: Archet: Theology vs. Mission

In this way, disagreement with the mission is considered an acceptable barrier of entry, but theological difference is considered less acceptable, albeit present. Therefore, if there is a differentiation for a person who comes to the church and has a stereotype of a church which does align with them as an individual, the degree to which the church finds this acceptable will depend on whether this is considered a theological difference or missional vision difference. Essentially, if a person attends and discovers that they are misaligned with an official theological stance of the church, the church leadership is prepared to trivialize traits and practices which would be salient for that individual. On the other hand, Archet Church would be less inclined to trivialize practices and traits which are currently being emphasized regarding their mission and vision.[10] As a clarifying reminder, these dots do not represent individuals per se, but traits, beliefs, or practices that come to be associated with some identity (or identities). Changes

---

10. Certainly, the exact nature of this emphasis is much more complex. For example, a church may—and likely is—more willing to trivialize some theological distinctions above others. This demonstrates the need for clarity from churches on these issues. Furthermore, there may be some individuals who do not find an identity becomes salient until they pursue further positions, as was the case with the individual from Koradai who did not believe in membership.

involving these dots will therefore affect different actual individuals differently. Overall, however, people will experience less (non-)belonging due to their distinctive theological convictions, but more (non-)belonging due to their acceptance or rejection of the community's mission. In other words, disagreement with the mission is considered an acceptable barrier that might prevent certain people from belonging, but theological differences are considered less acceptable barriers to entry.

Barriers to Belonging

In reflecting on barriers to belonging, there was a sense that Archet Church has dismantled a lot of barriers. There are some intergroup barriers which interviewees felt were unavoidable, saying, "There's the subtle barrier of being a church, so what does that mean and what do you do in there? How weird is it? But there's nothing forbidding or foreboding." By nature of being a church, this could present some barriers for individuals, but Archet seeks to eliminate as many unnecessary barriers as possible. Once again the open concept of the building was brought up as an asset. The front of the building has many windows, and there are not multiple layers of rooms to go through which creates a welcoming atmosphere. A member stated, "There's just one big place and you can either come and sit and kind of hide from everybody, or you can come walk around, drink coffee, and talk to everybody." Interestingly, another interviewee brought up this layout as a potential barrier to belonging, saying, "If [people] want to hide . . . they can't hide. We're in an open auditorium, like we're in an open room. There's not like a backseat. Right? Like there's, so you're pretty exposed no matter where you are. So that may prevent some people from trying it." In this, there may be a difference in normative fit for newcomers that is beneficial to the church, in that they would feel positively—i.e., "This is not what I thought a church was like!" Furthermore, the fact that comparatively there is similarity between the church and other environments such as a coffee shop may further reduce the sense of newcomers feeling like outsiders due to the casual environment which does not significantly differ from other environments said newcomers find themselves in. All interviewees felt that, overall, the layout promotes a friendly, casual, and inviting atmosphere. When asked what could be done to lower barriers, Chris, a leader in the church, stated,

> We can always be more visually accessible. We can always be more intentional in our communication to a broader set of the community. We, we can better represent the diversity in the community visually through, through who is, who is present on our social media, on our website, on stage, on a Sunday, the kind of things we promote. We could, we could, we could meet other additional needs. We have a free clothing store in the basement and so we have a lot of people come on Saturdays for that when it's open. But there's additional needs in the community that aren't just clothing that if we met those, we would be more accessible, I think, to a broader set of the community.

These factors reflect a parallel movement with both the contextual influence of the open environment and downtown space and the developed group identity of fostering intentional welcoming, both moving towards essential. The recent growth presents some practical limitations around space and logistically making sure people can come in and out of the building safely. There is an issue around seating due to the large growth, and there are questions around how to ensure that newcomers have a way to connect with other members of the church and the pastor. One source of weakness that was cited was around making connections to follow up with newcomers. However, it was suggested that this can be addressed by implementing a system for connecting newcomers with existing members and the pastor. This interviewee suggested that by assigning dedicated volunteers or staff members to personally reach out and follow up with newcomers, the church can ensure that newcomers welcomed and supported in their journey.

Factors of Belonging

One source reflected on their journey as a European immigrant coming to Canada when they were young and how this process shifted their perspective on belonging. Due to a number of factors including having a noticeable accent, being schooled with peers that were a different age, and a vastly different school culture, Steve reported that this shaped how he viewed belonging.

> And I think the unsettling of [that experience] that makes me the adult that I am, there's always this nagging thing in the back of my mind saying, "You don't really belong here." And it's not a conscious thought, but experiencing that, it's helpful and important for me to say, "Okay, where does that come from? I mean, do you

> belong here? How will you belong here? And what does it mean?" But it's that nagging suspicion that people are talking behind your back. So without paranoia it's just like, "Yeah, you really don't belong here." And I think the Christian sort of mandate and gospel mandate, it almost tells us that it's correct to think that way. So if I am in a, in a situation where it's all people who are not followers of Christ, like I have this bias that they don't really like me and wouldn't really like me because I really don't belong. And so some of that is proper, but some of it I think is dysfunctional.

Steve then expanded on this to reflect how the way he views those outside the church has changed. He explained that he used to have a bias towards non-Christians, feeling that they did not accept him because he did not belong. However, he acknowledged that this perspective was both proper and dysfunctional, as it prevented him from truly understanding and connecting with those outside the church. As he grew in his faith, Steve's mindset shifted, and he now approaches individuals from different beliefs with a more open and accepting attitude.

> I don't know why I would even have felt this way, but I grew up thinking that the people who don't go to church are "them" and they are bad. Then the other end of the pendulum swing is to say, no, we're all just the same and we're not, there's a proper distinction. But I think a healthy middle ground is to say we are the same. People are not—and this messes with my theology in my head—people are not essentially bad. Like, I think they're essentially good, but I'm not allowed to believe that. So that again kind of magnifies the "us/them" kind of a thing and say, "Well, if they were really good people, they would follow Jesus. They would come to church," and stuff like that.

Steve's comments reflect the desire to trivialize intergroup differentiation between the church and community. Due to stereotyping of those outside the church, he has experienced in the past a salient polarization between the church community and the world. He seeks to trivialize the practices and traits which in the past have emphasized this polarization. He suggests a correcting of the stereotype by which the comparative fit is shown to be aligned through commonality with community members. Through this reduction, a barrier of the congregants identity towards newcomers can be reduced.

Overall, the survey results reflected a higher degree of belonging at Archet church than in the average total. On average, the sense that it would be more difficult to leave the church was higher than average. Furthermore, there was a higher than average feeling of being an integral part of the community and feeling that the church community was "we" instead of "them." In comparing the subgroup identity scale of specific groups within the church, we see a lower than average degree of belonging among female members. Male members, Gen Z, and Gen X have a lower degree of belonging as well, and Baby Boomers have a higher degree of belonging than the average.

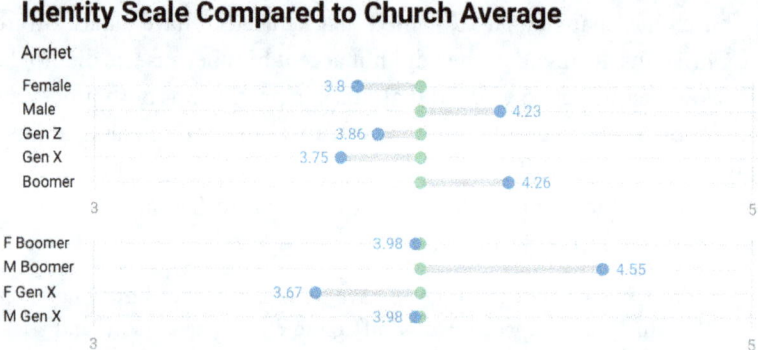

Figure 19: Survey Results: Identity Scale: Archet Average vs. Archet Subgroups

Out of this, there was interest in examining the identity scale for the following categories: male and female Boomers and male and female Gen X. As no female Gen Z respondents had completed the survey, I was not able to provide further comparative data on the Gen Z category. Furthermore, the overall survey does not have enough Gen Z respondents to provide meaningful comparative data across different churches. Nonetheless, this data helps to produce two key outliers in the identity scale, as shown in the second scale in figure 19. When compared to the church average, there was a high degree of belonging among male Boomers and a lower than average degree of belonging among female Gen X's. Overall in the survey data, we see a trend of higher shared identity among male members than female members. This reflects a very high degree of belonging among male members and a moderate sense of belonging among female members. The primary trends show that male Baby Boomers at Archet feel the most like they belong, while Gen X women feel less like they belong. Therefore, it would be of interest to explore further for church leadership as to the reasons behind this data. Unfortunately, due to low participation in interviews, there simply was not enough narrative data to draw any meaningful explanation as to why this pattern exists.

Regarding what it means for Archet Church to be a welcoming community, a theme emerged with Pastor Steve about removing the mentality that one is better than those outside of the church.

> We think we ought not to judge in the sense that we sort of stooped down to people. I think being a welcoming community says, "You look like me, you are like me and you're welcome to be here with me. So I'm not here to minister to you. I'm not here to condescend to you. I'm not here to power over you. . . . We respect you and we are not here to judge you." . . . Don't have a perception that people who are coming are either, you know, customers or possible converts.

Steve's remarks once again demonstrated his belief in reducing the intergroup salient comparative fit differentiation of outsiders into the church. Another pastor at the church remarked, "The culture of the space, culture of the people in the space, the energy, the temperament, like the character does feel, if I was to pick a church that I would just attend with my family, it would be this one, which tells me that it reflects my own identity in a dramatic way." In this comment, there is a sense of alignment in the normative fit between the pastor and the congregation The pastor sees himself as a stereotypical church member and hence as very closely aligned with the community's perceived identity.

Summary

Archet Church has a history of intentionality and community engagement. The downtown location of the church aims to keep it accessible and connected to the community, fostering stronger community engagement. Archet Church has been able to redefine its congregational identity and attract new members seeking spiritual fulfillment in recent years. The church seeks to build a strong community in which people can authentically support and encourage one another on their spiritual journeys. Archet Church continues to adapt to the changing needs of its congregation, attempting to remove barriers to belonging.

PHASE 3 PRESENTATION RESULTS

Church leadership provided positive feedback on the data, suggesting that it aided them to better understand their congregations.[11] As will be seen, some individuals found resonance in expressed thoughts and data, affirming pre-existing sentiments and knowledge. In contrast, others discovered previously unnoticed facets of their congregation's identity. This information also enabled church leaders to pinpoint areas of potential growth and enhancement within their congregation.

During the presentation of the data, Michael suggested that the data around church gatherings may have been more useful with a five point scale rather than a yes/no response. This clarifies the results with relevant details. In a subsequent chart, the yes/no responses were converted into binary inputs which were then separated to find average trends. Michael also found it interesting that church dinners and ministry teams were not a part of the response for Millennials/Gen Z female respondents. The binary scale of this question did indeed limit this data, and that is useful feedback for future research. Also, upon reflecting on this feedback, a grouped column was found to be more helpful with both gender and age groupings reflected in the same chart.

When reflecting on the identity scale, Michael stated, "We are not very balanced, it seems." He also summarized his understanding of the scale, saying, "So according to the scale, it seems that millennials have a strong identity with the church. And Gen Z is saying that they don't feel attached enough. No identity. . . . The identity scale that's pointing in the opposite direction, like Boomers, means that they don't have identity. They don't identify with the church." While it was clarified that the scale does not represent a binary identity/no identity scale, the understanding around the general meaning of the scale was accurate.

Pastors Steve and Michael both discussed the importance of language to categorize and understand concepts within the church context. Steve emphasized the need for a shared vocabulary within the church community to foster better communication and deeper understanding among its members. Additionally, Michael highlighted how language can shape our thoughts and beliefs, influencing our actions and attitudes towards various

---

11. On a personal note, I would like to thank again the church leaders for taking time to engage this material and applying it in real time to their own ministry context. Interplay with practice is essential for practical theological research, and the willingness to engage this content helped immensely.

topics within the church. Both pastors agreed that language plays a crucial role in facilitating meaningful discussions and fostering a strong sense of unity within the church.

Steve spoke about the way that exploring the survey results can address these issues in a less emotional way, allowing for a more objective and analytical approach. "If I lay [this framework] over things that we think about or talk about here, then it brings some clarity to be able to sort of categorize or sort things. Anytime you have language to talk about something that's not emotive or emotional, that's going to be helpful."

Similarly, Pastor Michael found the diagrams to be effective in communicating these complex social identity factors which happen in congregations.[12] He mentioned that the diagram provides a visual representation of the interconnectedness of these factors, allowing for a more objective and analytical approach to understanding them. This can facilitate productive discussions and problem solving within the congregation, promoting a deeper understanding and empathy among its members.

> I think it's an excellent diagram. With your permission, I'd like to use it in our church, just to give some understanding of where the church is going. It will simplify some of the thoughts because we have our half-year general meeting coming up in two weeks, and I'd like to do something in that meeting that will help people understand where we are and where we are going. That interchange is constantly there, and we need to live within that tension. You used that word earlier also. There's that constant tension of what was, what is, and what will be. On one hand, you have the constant tension of what is core, what is given, and what is chosen, and how those things can live with each other without causing major chaos within the church. I really like the diagram and its explanation. Makes a lot of sense.

John acknowledged the difficulty of defining terms such as "belonging" in the context of the church, saying, "One of the things, just as you define belonging, I'm aware in churches across the board, we talk about words like belonging and we have so many different meanings of what that is." The feedback also revealed John's thoughts on the impact of the research on the church, stating that it has helped in "identifying some issues—as we've talked about different things, [there are] ways for me to take action steps." John found the data to be extremely useful in communicating issues that he

---

12. The diagrams which Michael and the other pastors saw were earlier drafts of diagrams which appear here.

perceived to be widespread but that others did not believe. Even though the information given was not new to John, having tangible data in this form was beneficial to John. The data gave John a new perspective and validated his concerns, as he could see that others had similar concerns. This gave him comfort and confidence in addressing these issues within the church. Furthermore, the data enabled John to make a more compelling case to those who were skeptical or unaware of the issues, fostering a greater understanding and potential for change.

Due to the lower amount of narrative data from Archet Church, the degree of insights over the cause of certain survey results was limited. Nonetheless, despite the lack of available data to further explore these trends, during the presentation phase of the research, the pastor of Archet reflected that this was very useful information. As indicated in appendix 1, these comparative categories can be developed by churches to provide useful comparative data. While I was not able to provide him with data as to why these trends are present, he stated that this information is helpful to reflect on and provide deeper self-awareness of the congregation.

All three pastors who were interviewed emphasized the importance of exploring the topics of identity and belonging. There was an overall optimistic sense in the ability of these tools to assist, not only in solving these issues, but in providing greater awareness of the patterns which are emerging within congregations. The pastors believed that by delving into the topics of identity and belonging, congregations can foster a stronger sense of unity and inclusivity. They acknowledged that while these tools may not completely resolve all the challenges surrounding these issues, they have the ability to break apart assumptions which are often made about belonging. There was also a shared sense of the overall need of growth in the Canadian church in clarity over what it means to belong. There was a shared sense across all leaders that the tools employed in this research will be helpful in allowing church leaders to understand their congregation's complex identity and move forward with greater self-awareness.

CHAPTER 5

Conclusion

I AM CONCLUDING THIS research with a sense of excitement at the potential opportunities which may be available utilizing the tools formed in this research. I was surprised during the third phase of research to see the gratefulness which was expressed by all three pastors who were interviewed for this data and insight. There is also a sense of feeling overwhelmed, as I see the number of ways that concepts explored within this project may be useful to church leadership.

The survey responses produced a number of meaningful data points for the churches involved in the research. The Identity with a Group Scale is an excellent tool in defining reality in churches and finding these key insights. In the following appendix, I lay out a revised version of how a survey might be conducted to have more succinct and clear results. I suspect that as this is used, by myself or others, there will be further revisions to this scale. However, I am convinced that, in an effort to produce meaningful data from the complex organism that is the church, it is essential to accompany this with a deeper source of data such as narrative interviews. In chapter 1, we explored the fact that in the world of church leadership, we operate with past-centric or future-centric language, rarely entering into the present tense. This tool allows us to get a glimpse into the present tense of congregational identity.

Narrative interviews provide a more in-depth understanding of individuals' church experiences and perspectives, allowing for a more comprehensive analysis of the group's identity. This qualitative, conversational approach supplements the quantitative data gathered by the Identity with a Group Scale, improving overall understanding of reality within churches.

The limits of narrative data from Archet reflects the need for a diverse sample group for this type of research. Church leaders who wish to employ the type of research developed in this book will gain more valuable insights by gathering as large and diverse a sample as possible of interviewees. A diverse range of perspectives is required to provide a thorough description of a church. Conversely, the extensive input provided by Riverdale allowed a thorough narrative to be developed which in turn provided explanation for almost all data provided. Koradai church also had low turnout, but the extensive data provided by those interviewed helped to interpret the data. Furthermore, it is critical to ensure that the interview questions are carefully crafted in order to elicit rich and detailed responses from participants, thereby increasing the depth of understanding obtained through narrative interviews. I detail ways in which this may be done in appendix 1. In addition, including follow-up questions during the interview process can help clarify any ambiguous or incomplete responses, allowing for a more thorough analysis of the church's reality. There were times where an interviewee went into a long personal tangent which was irrelevant to the topic, but allowing this to play out then opened up an opportunity to later answer a relevant question. It is critical to create a safe and trusting environment in which participants can freely share their experiences and perspectives, as this can greatly contribute to the authenticity and richness of the information gathered.

The study's focus on a specific time period and the history of a church could be expanded to assess change over time through multiple comparative studies on a single congregation or community. For instance, a study spanning two years could explore how the transition from a male to a female pastor affects belonging across genders. A widespread analysis of belonging across Canadian churches could unveil meta factors across denominations, identifying emerging patterns and furthering research beneficial to churches. Furthermore, a study of one or several particular churches over a period of time or through a significant event would bring forth interesting data. Another aspect which can assist in future research is for church leaders to be engaged in shaping additional key questions for the Identity with a Group Scale in order to provide data which is relevant to specific issues of interest. This is explored further in the evaluation tool with suggestions on how church leaders may develop these questions in advance.

The "TEST" scale has been a useful tool for church leaders in fostering self-awareness of congregational identity. Church leaders can gain a

CONCLUSION

comprehensive understanding of the various factors that shape a church's identity by considering and even visualizing multiple perspectives. This allows them to understand aspects of social identity that they can directly influence as well as aspects they cannot. Church leaders can, to a certain extent, affect the perceived status of certain traits, beliefs, and practices; they have much less of an impact on the psychological salience of those same traits, beliefs, and practices. Furthermore, using narrative interviews allows for the exploration of personal experiences and emotions, providing valuable insights into community members' lived realities. This enables church leaders to be more self-aware of their communal identity. Using this model, church leaders can gain a better understanding of where the community has put up unknown barriers to belonging, allowing them to make informed decisions and implement effective growth and development strategies. Since this encourages active participation and engagement from all members in shaping the collective identity, this model fosters a sense of inclusivity and belonging within the church. This scale is particularly useful in exploring intragroup and intergroup differentiation and the potential for (non-)belonging that results from different overlapping social identities.

I have through this research become convinced that self-awareness of our communal identity is essential if we wish as churches to become places of belonging. All too often, church leaders—myself included—have simply stated what a church's identity is, and that we should be places of belonging, without realizing the full impact that our practices, traits, and beliefs have on one another. This reality was perhaps most succinctly stated by Pastor Steve during one of our interviews, when he said,

> The million dollar concern is belonging. It's what we all spend our lives either finding to be elusive or enticing. And I think many times we will market ourselves as churches on the basis of some language around belonging that turns out to be bullshit. But you know what you meant is, "Oh, you are all really good friends with each other, but you're gonna judge me. You're gonna exclude me and I'm really not welcome." So I think to just peel away the layers on that and say, quite honestly, this is the fundamental need that we all have—to belong. And surely the greatest promise of belonging is God's family. Where else would be a better place to find it?

As the church, our identity will continually be reframed in learning what it means to be the holy presence of God in this world, both distinct through holiness and radically present. The manner in which we do that is an ongoing work of discernment for the church.

This book began with reflections upon my journey of belonging within communities of faith, and it is there we return. As a pastor, I have the same tremendous concern about fostering places of belonging and being a welcoming community. I have a responsibility to be consciously aware of the individual characteristics of the people who attend the church I serve, as well as the collective characteristics of the church as a whole. I cannot simply make a statement to define who we are as a church, nor can I effectively lead if I do not understand the collective identity and story of the collective group I am serving, with all the messiness and complexity that comes with it.

Appendix

Evaluation Tool

THE NATURE OF CONDUCTING research such as identification with a group scale combined with narrative interviews on church communities is that there are certain elements which can only be learned through conducting the research. Through conducting this research, I believe that I have been able to refine the methodology of evaluation through observing areas of usefulness and areas which were not useful or needed refining. However, further research using these methods would likely further refine these tools. I believe that these tools are effective in their purpose, but they need to be adapted to fit in the specific needs of their users. In particular, the ability for congregations to formulate specific research questions with respect to distinctly *theological* beliefs and practices helps to expand the potential of the SIT tools as useful for the study of Christian congregations.

PHASE 1: DEVELOPMENT OF RESEARCH QUESTIONS AND SURVEY

Development of Research Questions

Here, questions which focus on deeper self-awareness will be developed. There are a variety of tools which can be employed to develop these questions, and the specific needs and structures of congregations, church leaders, and denominations will affect how these are developed. These may include questions of theological significance, since theology will often produce differentiation for religious people. This also may include questions that arise from a church's particular beliefs, practices, or traits. I have

Appendix

attempted to build this in a manner in which it is adaptable for a wide array of different contexts and practices within specific congregational contexts. Some examples are below; however, this list is not exhaustive, and care should be taken to develop questions in a manner which is appropriate for a particular context. Furthermore, ethical consideration should be taken in the tools employed. These can include:

- Asking congregants to put in anonymous submissions finishing the statement, "I wish I knew more about us as a church in the area of _____."
- Conducting preliminary interviews with members to determine areas where further awareness is helpful.
- Requesting live feedback during a church service on areas where further awareness would be helpful.
- Reflection during a leadership meeting or retreat on areas where further awareness is required.

It may be helpful at this point to also record the biases which are present. For example, if most church leaders believe that Gen Z members have a low sense of belonging to the church community, this should be recorded and referenced in developing the revised research question in phase 2, step 4.

Development of Survey

Section 1: Identification Scale

Question	Options
To what extent do you consider yourself an insider with respect to the community of <church name>?	Scale of 1–5, 1 being on the outside looking in, 5 being on the inside looking in
When you speak of the <church name> community, how often do you use "we" instead of "they"?	Never Rarely Sometimes Often Always
When you think of <church name>, do you feel you are an integral part of that community?	Yes No

How often do you see yourself as an outsider in <church name>?	Never Rarely Sometimes Often Always
To what extent do you agree/disagree with the following statement: I feel <church name>'s identity is aligned with my own identity.	1–5
Is being a part of <church name> a central part of your identity?	Never Rarely Sometimes Often Always
How difficult would it be to leave <church name>?	Scale 1–10
How important is being a part of <church name> to you?	Not important Somewhat important Important Very important I don't know

Section 2—Specific Questions

Here questions can be developed in accordance with the need for further self-awareness from a congregation, church leaders, denomination, etc. Below are some examples of research questions with comparative survey questions which can produce data in these areas.

Research Problem Examples	Survey Question(s)
We would like to know whether people who grew up in the church here have a deeper sense of belonging than newcomers.	How long have you attended <church name>?
We would like to know if second generation Canadians feel they are apart of our community as strongly as first generation Canadians.	Were you born in Canada? Were your parents born in Canada? (or, what country were you/your parents born in?)
We would like to know if unmarried adults in our church feel like outsiders	What is your marital status?

APPENDIX

Research Problem Examples	Survey Question(s)
We would like to know if our church feels open to a variety of political affiliations.	If you were to describe your political affiliation, how would you describe it? How comfortable are you being a part of a church community with those who have dramatically different political views?
We would like to know if those who fall outside of a particular ethnicity feel like outsiders.	What is your ethnicity? (or) Do you identify as (ethnicity)? yes/no
We would like to know how baptism affects the level of belonging church members feel	Have you been baptized? If yes, were you baptized at <church name> or another name?
We would like to know if church membership affects the level which someone feels apart of our church.	Are you a (registered, official, church, etc.) member of <church name>?
We would like to know if millennials feel like outsiders in our church.	What is your age?

As can be seen, the resulting survey questions are quite simple. It is important that the questions provide a specific clear data set. These questions then provide comparative matrices to interpret survey data and find patterns of belonging within a community of faith.

Section 3: Further Subgroup Data (optional)

This section can include questions which may not necessarily relate to specific research questions, but nonetheless may provide useful comparative data. Some of these questions may arise from the above research questions, some may not. Examples include:

What is your age?
What is your gender?
What is your ethnicity?
What is your marital status?
What is your country of origin?

This could also include questions specific to a church context, such as:

How much do value liturgy?

Evaluation Tool

How often do you attend church?
What worship style do you prefer?
What missional goal do you feel is most important?

Section 4: Revised Identification Questions (optional)

If a desired result of the survey is also to compare with identification of other groups people may be a part of, this can be done in this section through a revision of the questions in section 1. For example, if a church wished to know the level that their community identifies with their town or with a denomination, this could be done in this section. The following questions can be filled in with the appropriate group. Questions can be adjusted to be appropriate for the group being mentioned; however, care should be taken to preserve the wording as much as possible to provide useful comparative data with section 1.

Question	Options
To what extent do you consider yourself an insider with respect to the community of _____?	Scale of 1–5, 1 being on the outside looking in, 5 being on the inside looking in
When you speak of the _____ community, how often do you use "we" instead of "they"?	Never Rarely Sometimes Often Always
When you think of _____, do you feel you are an integral part of that community?	Yes No
How often do you see yourself as an outsider in _____?	Never Rarely Sometimes Often Always
To what extent to you agree/disagree with the following statement: I feel _____'s identity is aligned with my own identity.	1–5
Is being a part of _____ a central part of your identity?	Never Rarely Sometimes Often Always

Question	Options
How difficult would it be to leave_____?	Scale 1–10
How important is being a part of_____ to you?	Not important Some what important Important Very important I don't know

PHASE 2: CONDUCT AND SCORE SURVEY

Conduct Survey

In this phase, the researcher should conduct the survey in a manner which will maintain ethical distance between church leadership and identity of survey participants. This can be achieved by ensuring the anonymity and confidentiality of the survey responses. Additionally, it is important for the researcher to obtain informed consent from participants, clearly explaining the purpose and potential risks of the survey. Online resources are highly recommended to promote simplicity and anonymity, with paper options available. If paper copies are available, it is highly recommended to input these results into the online dataset. This will not only ensure the accuracy and consistency of the data but also make it easier to analyze and interpret. Furthermore, maintaining a secure and encrypted database for storing survey responses is crucial to protect the privacy of participants and prevent any unauthorized access or data breaches. Once survey is completed, the data should be converted into spreadsheet. This can be done automatically using most online survey platforms. Converting the data into a spreadsheet format allows for easier manipulation and organization of the information. This can facilitate further analysis and the creation of visualizations or reports based on the survey results.

Score Survey

Step 1: Convert Answers to Numerical Scores

Convert answers of survey identification questions to the following numerical values. This can be done through the spreadsheet of answers.

Evaluation Tool

Question	Options	Scoring Key	Highest Score
To what extent do you consider yourself an insider with respect to the community of <church name>?	Scale of 1–5, 1 being on the outside looking in, 5 being on the inside looking in	Enter Numerical Answer 1–5	5
When you speak of the <church name> community, how often do you use "we" instead of "they"?	Never Rarely Sometimes Often Always	Never=1 Rarely=2 Sometimes=3 Often=4 Always=5	5
When you think of <church name>, do you feel you are an integral part of that community?	Yes No	Yes=5 No=1	5
How often do you see yourself as an outsider in <church name>?	Never Rarely Sometimes Often Always	Never = 5 Rarely = 4 Sometimes = 3 Often = 2 Always = 1	5
To what extent to you agree / disagree with the following statement: I feel <church name>'s identity is aligned with my own identity.	1–5	Enter Numerical Answer 1–5	5
Is being a part of <church name> a central part of your identity?	Never Rarely Sometimes Often Always	Never = 1 Rarely = 2 Sometimes = 3 Often = 4 Always = 5	5
How difficult would it be to leave <church name>?	Scale 1–10	Enter Numerical Answer 1–10	10
How important is being a part of <church name> to you?	Not important Somewhat important Important Very important I don't know	Not important = 1 Somewhat important = 2 Important = 3 Very important = 4	4

For simplicity, it is possible to either have survey answers reflect the numerical values or convert the survey data manually using tools such as sorting tables.

Step 2: Create Identity Scale

Add total of each result. (Once again, this can be done directly in the spreadsheet).

Divide total score by forty-four. If any answers have no answer or state "prefer not to say," subtract the highest possible score for that question from forty-four and divide by that number. See above chart for highest possible score.

Multiply resulting score by five.

If other identification scales are a part of the research, the above skills should be repeated for those particular scales.

The result will be an individual score between one and five, representing the degree to which an individual feels a sense of belonging to that community.

Step 3: Produce Comparative Data

Averages within subcategories can be compared with total data averages or compared to one another. Some examples are below. This allows for a more detailed analysis and understanding of the variations within different subcategories. Additionally, comparing averages within subcategories can help identify trends or patterns that may not be apparent when looking at the total data averages alone. Some examples are below.

Survey Question(s)	Comparative Data Questions examples
How long have you attended <church name>	Which answers produce the highest and lowest identification scales?
Were you born in Canada? Were your parents born in Canada? (or, what country were you / your parents born in?)	What is the average identity scale of first, second, and third or further immigrants?

Evaluation Tool

Survey Question(s)	Comparative Data Questions examples
What is your marital status?	What is the identity scale average for those unmarried in comparison to those who are married?
If you were to describe your political affiliation, how would you describe it? How comfortable are you being a part of a church community with those who have dramatically different political views?	Are there consistent patterns with identity scales for those who identify as a particular political views?
What is your ethnicity? (or) Do you identify as (ethnicity) yes/no	Do those who represent a visible minority have a pattern of a different identity scale?

These questions will be shaped by the original research questions in order to disseminate the data to be useful in enhancing self-awareness for churches. By aligning the questions with the original research questions, the collected data can be effectively utilized to provide valuable insights for churches to enhance their self-awareness. This process of aligning the questions with the original research questions ensures that the data collected is relevant and directly contributes to improving self-awareness within churches. By analyzing this data, churches can gain a deeper understanding of their strengths, weaknesses, and areas for growth, ultimately leading to more informed decision-making and strategic planning.

Step 4: Develop Revised Research Questions Sourced from Survey Data

In this step, the research questions are revised to be reflective on what has been found thus far. For example,

Research Problem	We would like to know if unmarried adults in our church feel like outsiders.
Survey Question	What is your marital status?
Data Comparison Question	What is the identity scale average for those unmarried in comparison to those who are married?
Data Comparison Answer	Those unmarried and divorced have on average a lower identity scale than those who are married.

Revised Research Question	Why is there a lower sense of belonging among divorced and unmarried members compared to married members?

The revised research question should focus on objectively analyzing the data results and drawing conclusions based on empirical evidence. It should aim to uncover patterns, correlations, or trends within the data, without being influenced by personal biases or subjective opinions about the reasons behind those findings. Additionally, it is important for the research question to be framed in a way that allows for further exploration and investigation of potential causal relationships between variables identified in the data results. Therefore, if results are surprising, either positively or negatively, this should shape the direction of the revised research question. For example,

Research Problem	We would like to know if second generation Canadians feel they are a part of our community as strongly as first generation Canadians.
Survey Questions	Were you born in Canada? Were your parents born in Canada?
Data Comparison Question	What is the average identity scale of first, second, and third or further immigrants?
Data Comparison Answer	There was no noticeable pattern connecting levels of identity scales as it relates to generation of immigration.
Revised Research Question	Why is there not a significant difference of belonging based on being first or second generation immigrants?

PHASE 3: OBTAIN NARRATIVE INSIGHT INTO THE BACKGROUND OF DATA RESULTS

The survey provides a clear and precise set of data, allowing self-awareness into questions of who in a church feels like an outsider, who has a strong sense of belonging, and where some of these divides may fall. However, where this data lacks is providing the "why" to the data. For example, the survey data may provide a church clear data that young women have a very strong sense of belonging in the congregation but does not uncover why this is. Church leadership may also have ideas about the reason for factors, and although their input is important, it also carries certain bias. This is where narrative interviews can help to unpack the "why" of these factors.

Who Should Conduct Interviews?

It is not recommended that these narrative interviews be conducted by church leadership. Furthermore, while a member of the congregation may be able to effectively act in an appropriate arms-length manner while conducting the interviews, this creates a level of bias in the results, the potential risk based on interpersonal relationships, and the potential for inaccurate data based on the comfort level of people with someone who also knows theses situations. Therefore, the ideal person or group to conduct these interviews would be individuals who do not regularly attend that church or serve in a direct, ongoing leadership capacity. As a practitioner, I am empathetic to the practical issues which this limitation puts on the research. However, this is a necessary step in ensuring the resulting data is obtained ethically and is useful for advancing the self-awareness of the church community.

Interview Questions

The interview questions should be formed around two interconnected areas: the revised research question(s) and seeking a clarified metanarrative of the church community. Questions should be worded in a manner which promotes a narrative answer rather than a "Yes" or "No" answer. For example, rather than asking "Do you feel like an outsider because of your ethnicity?" one could ask "Could you share a bit about your story with how your ethnicity has interacted with being a part of a church community?" Interviews should then be transcribed, anonymized, and sorted to reflect the various responses given to the questions. From this, a summary can be provided.

From this, findings can be produced. The findings should not report on data which does not exist—for example, if a clear answer to the revised research question was not found, then that is part of the findings. However, what was found can be reported, even if it was a partial answer or the information invokes further questions. For example,

Research Problem	We would like to know if those who fall outside of a particular ethnicity feel like outsiders.
Survey Questions	What is your ethnicity?
Data Comparison Question	Do those who represent a visible minority have a pattern of a different identity scale?
Data Comparison Answer	Those who did not identify as white had a lower average identity scale than those who were white.
Revised Research Question	What factors contribute to a lower sense of belonging for visible minorities in our congregation?
Findings	Visible minorities have a stronger sense of belonging when there is visible diversity in leadership. Many white members of the congregation feel a sense of not knowing how to interact with visible minorities appropriately. Existing narratives of the formation of the church are interconnected with Anglo-Saxon immigration, and it is difficult for members from visible minorities to feel a part of the church's history.

PHASE 4: REFLECT ON FINDINGS

During this phase, church leadership can reflect on the factors which relate to these identities and whether these would be categorized and how intentional and essential they are. Furthermore, reflection on where there is dissonance between what one might feel ought to be in one category but seems to be in another is important. This reflection allows church leadership to gain a deeper self-awareness of the congregation's values and beliefs, as well as how these identities influence their decision-making processes. By recognizing any dissonance between the expected and actual categorization of identities, church leadership can work towards aligning them more effectively with the overall mission and vision of the church. Additionally, this phase presents an opportunity for leaders to engage in open dialogue with the congregation, fostering a sense of inclusivity and ensuring that everyone's perspectives are considered. As an example, a church leadership may feel that a certain identity is an intentional category which is trivial, but the data reflects a chosen identity close to essential. By understanding this reality, this can inform the church leadership both in helping to define the actual identity and access future visions and goals. At this point, they can begin mapping these identities with the degree of salient differentiation and trivialization or emphasis creating various comparative TEST scales. These scales can compare current to ideal and past to present and also explore how shifts in trivialization and emphasis will influence intergroup and intragroup belonging.

Out of this, the church leadership can begin to reflect on where trivialization and emphasis can move. They can reflect on ways in which salient differentiation causes belonging and non-belonging and how comparative fit, normative fit, and perceiver readiness determine whether these identities align with the shared mission and vision of the church. Furthermore, they can reflect on the identities revealed through these studies and how trivialization or emphasis may impact this.

Bibliography

"2001 Community Profiles." Statistics Canada, July 2, 2019. https://www12.tatcan.c.a/english/profilo1/cpo1/details/page.fm?lang=eandgeo1=csdandcode1=3524015andgeo2=prandcode2=35anddata=countandsearchtext=halton%20hillsandsearchtype=beginsandsearchpr=01andb1=allandcustom=.

Abrams, Dominic, and Michael A. Hogg. "Social Identification, Self-Categorization and Social Influence." *European Review of Social Psychology* 1 (1990) 195–228.

———. "Social Identity and Self-Categorization." In *The SAGE Handbook of Prejudice, Stereotyping and Discrimination*, by John Dovidio et al., 179–93. London: SAGE, 2010.

Alexander, Stacia. "Examining the Retention of African American Young Adults in Their Childhood Church." PhD diss., Amberton University, 2017.

Allen, Kelly-Ann, et al. "Belonging: A Review of Conceptual Issues, an Integrative Framework, and Directions for Future Research." *Australian Journal of Psychology* 73 (2021) 87–102.

Ammerman, Nancy T. *Sacred Stories, Spiritual Tribes: Finding Religion in Everyday Life.* Oxford: Oxford University Press, 2013.

———. "Spiritual but Not Religious? Beyond Binary Choices in the Study of Religion." *Journal for the Scientific Study of Religion* 52 (2013) 258–78.

———. "Spiritual Narratives in Everyday Life." Institute on Culture, Religion and World Affairs, Boston University, 2013. https://www.bu.edu/sociology/files/2013/02/Spiritual-Narratives-in-Everyday-Life.pdf.

Ammerman, Nancy T., and Roman R. Williams. "Speaking of Methods: Eliciting Religious Narratives Through Interviews, Photos, and Oral Diaries." *Annual Review of the Sociology of Religion* 3 (2012) 117–34.

Anderson, Herbert, and Edward Foley. *Mighty Stories, Dangerous Rituals: Weaving Together the Human and the Divine.* Hoboken, NJ: Jossey-Bass, 2001.

Anderson, Wes, dir. *Fantastic Mr. Fox.* 20th Century Fox, 2009.

Arnsperger, Christian, and Yanis Varoufakis. "Toward a Theory of Solidarity." *Erkenntnis* 59 (2003) 157–88.

Ashforth, Blake E., and Fred Mael. "Social Identity Theory and the Organization." *Academy of Management Review* 14 (1989) 20–39.

Athanasius. *On the Incarnation.* Translated by John Behr. Yonkers, NY: St Vladimir's Seminary Press, 2011.

Baker, Coleman A. *Identity, Memory, and Narrative in Early Christianity: Peter, Paul, and Recategorization in the Book of Acts.* Eugene, OR: Wipf & Stock, 2011.

———. "Social Identity Theory and Biblical Interpretation." *Biblical Theology Bulletin* 42 (2012) 129–38.

Barentsen, Jack. "Apostasy: A Social Identity Perspective." In *Religiously Exclusive, Socially Inclusive? A Religious Response*, edited by Bernhard Reitsma and Erika van Nes-Visscher, 59–73. Amsterdam: Amsterdam University Press, 2023.

———. "Church Leadership as Adaptive Identity Construction in a Changing Social Context." *Journal of Religious Leadership* 15 (2015) 49–80.

———. "Understanding Peace and Conflict Through Social Identity Theory: Contemporary Global Perspectives." *Practical Theology* 10 (2017) 321–22.

Bartholomä, Philipp F. "The Ecclesiological Self and the Other: Concepts of Social Identity and Their Implications for Free Churches in Secular Europe." *Ecclesial Practices* 2 (2015) 156–76.

Bass, Dorothy C., and Craig R. Dykstra. *For Life Abundant: Practical Theology, Theological Education, and Christian Ministry*. Grand Rapids: Eerdmans, 2008.

Baumeister, Roy F., and Mark R. Leary. "The Need to Belong: Desire for Interpersonal Attachments as a Fundamental Human Motivation." *Psychological Bulletin* 117 (1995) 497–529.

Baxter, Anthony. "Holiness and Sin." *New Blackfriars* 70 (1989) 506–17.

Beach, Lee, *The Church in Exile: Living in Hope After Christendom*. Downers Grove, IL: IVP Academic, 2015.

Beattie, Laura Jean. "The Ethnic Church and Immigrant Integration: Social Services, Cultural Preservation and the Re-Definition of Cultural Identity." MA thesis, University of British Columbia, 1998.

Blanz, Mathias, and Birgit Aufderheide. "Social Categorization and Category Attribution: The Effects of Comparative and Normative Fit on Memory and Social Judgment." *British Journal of Social Psychology* 38 (1999) 157–79.

Bond, Edward U. "Antecedents of Member Commitment to the Local Church." *Journal of Ministry Marketing and Management* 7 (2002) 35–49.

Borwein, Sophie, and Jack Lucas. "Municipal Identity and City Interests." *Political Behavior* 45 (2023) 877–96.

Botros, Ghada. "Religious Identity as an Historical Narrative: Coptic Orthodox Immigrant Churches and the Representation of History." *Journal of Historical Sociology* 19 (2006) 174–201.

Bravata, Dena, et al. "Commentary: Prevalence, Predictors, and Treatment of Imposter Syndrome: A Systematic Review." *Journal of General Internal Medicine* 4 (2020) 12–16.

Brenner, Philip S., et al. "The Causal Ordering of Prominence and Salience in Identity Theory: An Empirical Examination." *Social Psychology Quarterly* 77 (2014) 231–52.

Brewer, Marilynn B., and Kathleen P. Pierce. "Social Identity Complexity and Outgroup Tolerance." *Personality and Social Psychology Bulletin* 31 (2005) 428–37.

Brewer, Marilynn B., and W. Gardner, "Who Is This 'We'? Levels of Collective Identity and Self Representations." *Journal of Personality and Social Psychology* 71 (1996) 83–93.

Brown, Rupert. *Henri Tajfel: Explorer of Identity and Difference*. New York: Routledge, 2019.

Busetto, Loraine, et al. "How to Use and Assess Qualitative Research Methods." *Neurological Research and Practice* 2 (2020) 1–10.

Byars, Ronald P. *The Future of Protestant Worship: Beyond the Worship Wars*. Louisville: Westminster John Knox, 2002.

Bibliography

Campbell, David E. "Acts of Faith: Churches and Political Engagement." *Political Behavior* 26 (2004) 155–80.

Candy, Linda. "Practice Based Research: A Guide." *CCS Report* 1 (2006) 1–19.

Cantor, Nancy, et al. "On Motivation and the Self-Concept." In *Handbook of Motivation and Cognition: Foundations of Social Behavior*, edited by Richard M. Sorrentino and E. Tory Higgins, 96–121. New York: Guilford, 1986.

Capozza, Dora, and Rupert Brown. *Social Identity Processes: Trends in Theory and Research*. London: SAGE, 2000.

Capps, Donald. *The Decades of Life: A Guide to Human Development*. Louisville: Westminster John Knox, 2008.

Carr, David. "Narrative and the Real World: An Argument for Continuity." *History and Theory* 25 (1986) 117–31.

Cinnirella, Marco. "Exploring Temporal Aspects of Social Identity: The Concept of Possible Social Identities." *European Journal of Social Psychology* 28 (1998) 227–48.

Clandinin, D. Jean. *Handbook of Narrative Inquiry: Mapping a Methodology*. London: SAGE, 2007.

Clark, Chap, and Steven Argue. *Adoptive Church: Creating an Environment Where Emerging Generations Belong*. Grand Rapids: Baker Academic, 2018.

Clark, Warren. "Pockets of Belief: Religious Attendance Patterns in Canada." *Canadian Social Trends* 68 (2003) 2–5.

Clarke, Brian, and Stuart Macdonald. *Leaving Christianity: Changing Allegiances in Canada Since 1945*. Montreal: McGill-Queen's University Press, 2017.

Clements, Ronald Ernest. *God and Temple: The Idea of the Divine Presence in Ancient Israel*. Eugene, OR: Wipf & Stock, 2016.

Connelly, F. Michael, and D. Jean Clandinin. "Stories of Experience and Narrative Inquiry." *Educational Researcher* 19 (1990) 2–14.

Conradie, E. M. *Christian Identity: An Introduction*. Stellenbosch: SUN PReSS, 2005.

Cook, Ryan. "Social Identity in Crisis: Toward a Theology of the Psalms of Asaph." *The Asbury Theological Journal* 77 (2022) 245–66.

Cornelissen, Louis. "Religiosity in Canada and Its Evolution from 1985 to 2019." Statistics Canada, Oct. 28, 2021. https://www150.tatcan.c.a/n1/pub/75-006-x/2021001/article/00010-eng.tm.

Crabtree, Noah. "The Prophet from Anathoth: Benjamin-Judean Identity Negotiation and the Formation of the Book of Jeremiah." PhD diss., Johns Hopkins University, 2023.

Crites, Stephen. "The Narrative Quality of Experience." *Journal of the American Academy of Religion* 39 (1971) 291–311.

Dewell, Justin B. "Known as Servants: Social Identity Theory and Mark 10:35–45." Paper presented at the Stone-Campbell Journal Conference, April 4–5, 2019.

Diamant, Sarah. "Group Identity in the Hebrew Bible: Moab as a Case of Israelite Self-Identity." PhD diss., The Jewish Theological Seminary, 2008.

Dickie, J. "Building Community in the Church Between Insiders and Outsiders." *Acta Theologica* 40 (2020) 50–68.

Dowdle, Sondra Robertson. "Disaffection in Southern Baptist Churches: Perspectives of the Marginalized." PhD diss., Mississippi State University, 2018.

Dunlop, Andrew. "Using the 'Four Voices of Theology' in Group Theological Reflection." *Practical Theology* 14 (2021) 294–308.

Du Toit, Philip La G. "Rethinking Identity Theory in Light of the In-Christ Identity in the African Context." *HTS Teologiese Studies* 80 (2024) 1–9.

Bibliography

Duval, Shelley, and Robert A. Wicklund. *A Theory of Objective Self Awareness*. Oxford: Academic, 1972.

Ervin, Laurie H., and Sheldon Stryker. "Theorizing the Relationship Between Self-Esteem and Identity." In *Extending Self-Esteem Theory and Research: Sociological and Psychological Currents*, edited by Timothy J. Owens et al., 29–55. Cambridge: Cambridge University Press, 2001.

Esler, Philip F. "Conflict: the Parable of the Good Samaritan Jesus and the Reduction of Intergroup in the Light of Social Identity Theory." *Biblical Interpretation* 8 (2000) 325–57.

———. "'Keeping It in the Family': Culture, Kinship and Identity in 1 Thessalonians and Galatians." In *Families and Family Relations*, edited by Athalya Brenner and Jan Willem van Henten, 145–84. Boston: Brill, 2001.

———. "Paul's Explanation of Christ-Movement Identity in 2 Corinthians 6:14—7:1: A Social Identity Approach." *Biblical Theology Bulletin* 51 (2021) 101–18.

———. "Social Identity, the Virtues, and the Good Life: A New Approach to Romans 12: 1—15:13." *Biblical Theology Bulletin* 33 (2003) 51–63.

Estes, Thomas W. "A Seminarian's Word: The Power of a Name: Ingroups, Outgroups, and Canonical Imagination." *Review and Expositor* 114 (2017) 18–22.

Ete, Ziya, et al. "Leader and Organizational Behavioral Integrity and Follower Behavioral Outcomes: The Role of Identification Processes." *Journal of Business Ethics* 176 (2022) 741–60.

Fee, Gordon D. "Εἰδωλόθυτα Once Again: An Interpretation of 1 Corinthians 8–10." *Biblica* 61 (1980) 172–197.

Ferguson, Neil. *Practice-Led Theology: A Model for Faith-Based Research*. Eugene, OR: Wipf & Stock, 2024.

Fillery-Travis, Annette, and Linda Robinson. "Making the Familiar Strange—A Research Pedagogy for Practice." *Studies in Higher Education* 43 (2018) 841–53.

Fitch, David E. *The Church of Us vs. Them: Freedom from a Faith That Feeds on Making Enemies*. Grand Rapids: Brazos, 2019.

Frable, D. E., et al. "Marginal and Mindful: Deviants in Social Interactions." *Journal of Personality and Social Psychology* 59 (1990) 140–49.

Fretz, J. Winfield. *The Waterloo Mennonites: A Community in Paradox*. Waterloo, ON: Wilfrid Laurier University Press, 2010.

Fuller, Tyler J., et al. "Re-Membering HIV in the Black Church: Women's Religious and Social Identity in Relation to Perceived Risk and Men on the Down Low." *Culture, Health and Sexuality* 24 (2022) 437–50.

Gammie, John G. *Holiness in Israel*. Eugene, OR: Wipf & Stock, 2005.

Ganzevoort, R. Ruard. "Narrative Approaches." In *The Wiley-Blackwell Companion to Practical Theology*, edited by Bonnie J. Miller-McLemore, 214–23. Wiley-Blackwell Companions to Religion. Malden, MA: Wiley-Blackwell, 2012.

Gerkin, Charles V. *Widening the Horizons: Pastoral Responses to a Fragmented Society*. Philadelphia: Westminster John Knox, 1986.

Gill, Robin. *Changing Worlds: Can the Church Respond?* London: Bloomsbury, 2002.

———. "The Cultural Paradigm: Declines in Belonging and Then Believing." In *The Role of Religion in Modern Societies*, edited by Daniel V. A. Olson and Detlef Pollack, 183–95. New York: Routledge, 2008.

Gray, Carole. "From the Ground Up: Encountering Theory in the Process of Practice led Doctoral Research." In *Theory? Encounters with Theory in Practice-Based PhD*

Research in Art and Design, AHRC Postgraduate Conference, De Montfort University & Loughborough Universities, UK. June 26, 2007.

Greenfield, Emily A., and Nadine E. Marks. "Religious Social Identity as an Explanatory Factor for Associations Between More Frequent Formal Religious Participation and Psychological Well-Being." *The International Journal for the Psychology of Religion* 17 (2007) 245–59.

Gustafson, David M. "Evangelists of Church History: Wisdom for Evangelism in Western Contexts Today." *Post-Christendom Studies* 5 (2020) 5–32.

Habib, Sadia, and Michael Ward, eds. *Youth, Place and Theories of Belonging*. New York: Routledge, 2019.

Hafer, Joseph, et al. "Editorial: Social Identity Dynamics in a Networked Society." *Frontiers in Psychology* 14 (2023) 1264534.

Hagerty, B. M., et al. "Sense of Belonging: A Vital Mental Health Concept." *Archives of Psychiatric Nursing* 6 (1992) 172–77.

Hakola, Raimo. "Social Identities and Group Phenomena in Second Temple Judaism." In *Explaining Christian Origins and Early Judaism*, edited by Petri Luomanen et al., 259–76. Leiden: Brill, 2007.

Hannum, Kelly M. *Social Identity: Knowing Yourself, Knowing Others*. Hoboken, NJ: Wiley, 2011.

Haslam, Catherine, et al. "Identity, Influence, and Change: Rediscovering John Turner's Vision for Social Psychology." *British Journal of Social Psychology* 51 (2012) 201–18.

Haslam, Catherine, et al. "'When the Age Is in, the Wit Is Out': Age-Related Self-Categorization and Deficit Expectations Reduce Performance on Clinical Tests Used in Dementia Assessment." *Psychology and Aging* 27 (2012) 778–84.

Haslam, S. Alexander, et al. *The New Psychology of Leadership: Identity, Influence and Power*. 2nd ed. New York: Routledge, 2020.

Hauerwas, Stanley. *Character and the Christian Life*. Notre Dame: University of Notre Dame Press, 1994.

Hauerwas, Stanley, and L. Gregory Jones. *Why Narrative? Readings in Narrative Theology*. Eugene, OR: Wipf & Stock, 1989.

Heesing, Matthew J. "A Denomination's Dealings with Difference: Considering Recategorization and Mutual Intergroup Differentiation in the Context of the United Church of Canada." MA thesis, Saint Mary's University, 2015.

Hemler, Jonathan J. "American Faith Adrift: The Rise of Religious Nones and the Influence of Political Polarization." MA thesis, Johns Hopkins University, 2020.

Herl, Joseph. *Worship Wars in Early Lutheranism: Choir, Congregation, and Three Centuries of Conflict*. Oxford: Oxford University Press, 2004.

Herriot, Peter. *Religious Fundamentalism and Social Identity*. New York: Routledge, 2007.

Himmelweit, H. T. "Obituary: Henri Tajfel, FBPsS." *Bulletin of the British Psychological Society* 35 (1982) 288–89.

Ho, Sin Pan Daniel. "'Cleanse Out the Old Leaven, That You May Be a New Lump': A Rhetorical Analysis of 1 Cor 5–11: 1 in Light of the Social Lives of the Corinthians." PhD diss., University of Sheffield, 2012.

———. *Paul and the Creation of a Counter-Cultural Community: A Rhetorical Analysis of 1 Cor. 5.1—11.1 in Light of the Social Lives of the Corinthians*. London: T&T Clark, 2015.

Hogg, Michael A. "Group Cohesiveness: A Critical Review and Some New Directions." *European Review of Social Psychology* 4 (1993) 85–111.

———. "Social Identity: The Role of Self in Group Processes and Intergroup Relations." *Group Processes and Intergroup Relations* 20 (2017) 570–81.

———. "Subjective Uncertainty Reduction Through Self-Categorization: A Motivational Theory of Social Identity Processes." *European Review of Social Psychology* 11 (2000) 223–55.

Hogg, Michael A., and Scott A. Reid. "Social Identity, Leadership, and Power." In *The Use and Abuse of Power: Multiple Perspectives on the Causes of Corruption*, edited by A. Y. Lee-Chai and J. A. Bargh, 159–80. Philadelphia: Psychology Press, 2001.

Hogg, Michael A., et al. "Intergroup Leadership in Organizations: Leading Across Group and Organizational Boundaries." *Academy of Management Review* 37 (2012) 232–55.

———. "The Social Identity Theory of Leadership: Theoretical Origins, Research Findings, and Conceptual Developments." *European Review of Social Psychology* 23 (2012) 258–304.

Hopewell, James F. *Congregation: Stories and Structures*. Philadelphia: Fortress, 1987.

Horrell, David G. *Solidarity and Difference: A Contemporary Reading of Paul's Ethics*. London: Bloomsbury Academic, 2005.

———. "Solidarity and Difference: Pauline Morality in Romans 14:1—15:13." *Studies in Christian Ethics* 15 (2002) 60–78.

Hostetler, Beulah Stauffer. *American Mennonites and Protestant Movements: A Community Paradigm*. Kitchener, ON: Herald, 2018.

Hout, Michael, and Claude S. Fischer. "Why More Americans Have No Religious Preference: Politics and Generations." *American Sociological Review* 67 (2002) 165–90.

Huddy, Leonie, and Nadia Khatib. "American Patriotism, National Identity, and Political Involvement." *American Journal of Political Science* 51 (2007) 63–77.

Huddy, Leonie, et al. "Expressive Partisanship: Campaign Involvement, Political Emotion, and Partisan Identity." *American Political Science Review* 109 (2015) 1–17.

Johnson, Terri L. "Worship Styles, Music and Social Identity: A Communication Study." MA thesis, Cleveland State University, 2006.

Kaiser, Karen. "Protecting Respondent Confidentiality in Qualitative Research." *Qualitative Health Research* 19 (2009) 1632–41.

Kang, Ezer. "Human Immunodeficiency Virus (HIV) Stigma: Spoiled Social Identity and Jürgen Moltmann's Trinitarian Model of the Imago Dei." *International Journal of Public Theology* 9 (2015) 289–312.

Karpa, Jane V. "Narrative Inquiry Methodology and Family Research: An Innovative Approach to Understanding Acquired Brain Injuries." *International Journal of Qualitative Methods* 20 (2021) 160940692110217.

Kim, Jeong-Hee. *Understanding Narrative Inquiry: The Crafting and Analysis of Stories as Research*. Thousand Oaks: SAGE, 2015.

Kwon, Ho-Youn. *Korean Americans and Their Religions: Pilgrims and Missionaries from a Different Shore*. University Park: Pennsylvania State University Press, 2010.

Langdridge, Darren. "Sadism/Masochism." In *Encyclopedia of Critical Psychology*, edited by Thomas Teo, 1687–90. New York: Springer, 2014.

Lane, Erin. *Lessons in Belonging from a Church-Going Commitment Phobe*. Downers Grove, IL: InterVarsity, 2015.

Lau, Peter H. W. *Identity and Ethics in the Book of Ruth: A Social Identity Approach*. Berlin: de Gruyter, 2011.

Bibliography

Lee, Daniel. *Old Order Mennonites: Rituals, Beliefs, and Community.* Chicago: Rowman and Littlefield, 2000.

Lickel, Brian, et al. "Elements of a Lay Theory of Groups: Types of Groups, Relational Styles, and the Perception of Group Entitativity." *Personality and Social Psychology Review* 5 (2001) 129–40.

Lipka, Michael. "5 Facts About Religion in Canada." Pew Research Center, July 1, 2019. https://www.pewresearch.org/short-reads/2019/07/01/5-facts-about-religion-in-canada/.

Mael, Fred A., and Lois E. Tetrick. "Identifying Organizational Identification." *Educational and Psychological Measurement* 52 (1992) 813–24.

Markus, Hazel, and Paula Nurius. "Possible Selves." *American Psychologist* 41 (1986) 954–69.

Mascareño, Aldo, and Fabiola Carvajal. "The Different Faces of Inclusion and Exclusion." *CEPAL Review* 2015 (2016) 127–41.

May, Alistair Scott. "The Body for the Lord: Sex and Identity in 1st Corinthians 5–7." PhD diss., University of Glasgow, 2001.

McCall, George J., and J. L. Simmons. *Identities and Interactions.* New York: Free Press, 1966.

McGarty, Craig. *Categorization in Social Psychology.* London: SAGE, 1999.

McMillan, David W., and David M. Chavis. "Sense of Community: A Definition and Theory." *Journal of Community Psychology* 14 (1986) 6–23.

McNamara, Andrew. "Six Rules for Practice-led Research." *Journal of Writing and Writing Courses* 14 (2012) 1–15.

Mercer, Joyce Ann, and Bonnie Miller-McLemore. *Conundrums in Practical Theology.* Theology in Practice 2. Boston: Brill, 2016.

Miller, Donald. *Building a StoryBrand: Clarify Your Message So Customers Will Listen.* New York: HarperCollins Leadership, 2017.

Miller-McLemore, Bonnie J. *Christian Theology in Practice: Discovering a Discipline.* Grand Rapids: Eerdmans, 2012.

———. "Five Misunderstandings About Practical Theology." *International Journal of Practical Theology* 16 (2012) 5–26.

———. *The Wiley-Blackwell Companion to Practical Theology.* Wiley-Blackwell Companions to Religion. Malden, MA: Wiley-Blackwell, 2012.

Mok, Carson Ka Shing. "Congregational Singing as Social Identity Shaping in Toronto Cantonese Worship Services." DPT diss., McMaster Divinity College, 2023.

Morin, Alain. "Self-Awareness Part 1: Definition, Measures, Effects, Functions, and Antecedents." *Social and Personality Psychology Compass* 5 (2011) 807–23.

Mowday, R. T., et al. "The Measurement of Organizational Commitment." *Journal of Vocational Behavior* 14 (1979) 224–47.

Myers, Joseph R., et al. *The Search to Belong: Rethinking Intimacy Community and Small Groups.* Grand Rapids: Zondervan, 2003.

Nebreda, Sergio Rosell. *Christ Identity: A Social-Scientific Reading of Philippians 2.5–11.* Göttingen: Vandenhoeck and Ruprecht, 2011.

Nell, Ian A. "Preaching as Self-Categorisation: Analyzing a Beyers Naudé Sermon by Making Use of Social Identity Theory." *Nederduitse Gereformeerde Teologiese Tydskrif* 54 (2013) 119–30.

O'Neil, Michael D. "The Role of Baptism in Christian Identity Formation." *Religions* 15 (2024) 458–80.

Bibliography

O'Reilly, Michelle, and Nicola Parker. "'Unsatisfactory Saturation': A Critical Exploration of the Notion of Saturated Sample Sizes in Qualitative Research." *Qualitative Research* 13 (2013) 190–97.

Osmer, Richard Robert. *Practical Theology: An Introduction*. Grand Rapids: Eerdmans, 2008.

Packard, Josh, and Todd W. Ferguson. "Being Done: Why People Leave the Church, but Not Their Faith." *Sociological Perspectives* 62 (2019) 499–517.

Patrikios, Stratos. "Self-Stereotyping as 'Evangelical Republican': An Empirical Test." *Politics and Religion* 6 (2013) 800–822.

Pinto, Isabel R., et al. "Membership Status and Subjective Group Dynamics: Who Triggers the Black Sheep Effect?" *Journal of Personality and Social Psychology* 99 (2010) 107–19.

Pogue, Alan Lewis. "Communicating Identity: Communication Processes in the Development of Group Identity Through Congregational Worship Rituals." PhD diss., University of Oklahoma, 2002.

Polkinghorne, Donald E. *Narrative Knowing and the Human Sciences*. Albany, NY: State University of New York Press, 1988.

Porter, Christopher A., and Brian S. Rosner. "'All Things to All People': 1 Corinthians, Ethnic Flexibility, and Social Identity Theory." *Currents in Biblical Research* 19 (2021) 286–307.

Power, Georja Jane. "Organizational, Professional and Personal Roles in an Era of Change: The Case of the Catholic Clergy." PhD diss., Australian Catholic University, 2003.

"Profile Table, Census Profile, 2021 Census of Population-Halton Hills, Town (T) [Census Subdivision], Ontario." Statistics Canada, Feb 9, 2022. https://www12.tatcan.c.a/census-recensement/2021/dp-pd/prof/index.fm?Lang=E.

Punt, Jeremy. "Post-Apartheid Racism in South Africa The Bible, Social Identity and Stereotyping." *Religion and Theology* 16 (2008) 246–72.

Richardson, Cyril C. *Early Christian Fathers*. New York: MacMillan, 2006.

Reed, Randall W. "Emerging Treason? Politics and Identity in the Emerging Church Movement." *Critical Research on Religion* 2 (2014) 66–85.

Regehr, T. D. *Mennonites in Canada, 1939-1970: A People Transformed*. University of Toronto Press, 1996.

Roberts, Robert C. *Spiritual Emotions: A Psychology of Christian Virtues*. Grand Rapids: Eerdmans, 2007.

Rosell Nebreda, Sergio. *Christ Identity: A Social-Scientific Reading of Philippians 2–11*. Göttingen: Vandenhoeck & Ruprecht, 2011.

Ruth, Lester. "The Eruption of Worship Wars: The Coming of Conflict." *Liturgy* 32 (2017) 3–6.

Salzman, P. C. "On Reflexivity." *American Anthropologist* 104 (2002) 805–13.

Sapolu, Pasesa. "Reconciling Identities: Social Identity, Hybridity, and Leadership in the Nehemiah Memoir." PhD diss., Graduate Theological Union, 2020.

Schell, Maximilian. "Gruppe und Identität: Der Social Identity Approach im Gespräch mit theologischer Anthropologie und Ethik." *Evangelische Theologie* 81 (2021) 51–64.

Seal, Darlene M. "'These Things Were Written for Us': Scriptural Re-Interpretation and Social Creativity in the Corinthian Letters." PhD diss., McMaster Divinity College, 2022.

Sedikides, Constantine, et al. *Intergroup Cognition and Intergroup Behavior*. Applied Social Research. New York: Routledge, 1998.

Seiple, Robert A. "From Bible Bombardment to Incarnational Evangelism: A Reflection on Christian Witness and Persecution." *The Review of Faith and International Affairs* 7 (2009) 29–37.

Sewell, David K., et al. "Exemplifying 'Us': Integrating Social Identity Theory of Leadership with Cognitive Models of Categorization." *The Leadership Quarterly* 33 (2022) 101517.

Singfiel, Jeff. "When Servant Leaders Appear Laissez-Faire: The Effect of Social Identity Prototypes on Christian Leaders." *Journal of Applied Christian Leadership* 12 (2018) 64–77.

Smucker, Joseph. "Religious Community and Individualism: Conceptual Adaptations by One Group of Mennonites." *Journal for the Scientific Study of Religion* 25 (1986) 273–91.

Stargel, Linda M. *The Construction of Exodus Identity in Ancient Israel: A Social Identity Approach.* Eugene, OR: Wipf & Stock, 2018.

Steffens, Niklas K., et al. "Leadership as Social Identity Management: Introducing the Identity Leadership Inventory (ILI) to Assess and Validate a Four-Dimensional Model." *Leadership Quarterly* 25 (2014) 1001–24.

Steffens, Niklas K., et al. "Social Identity Mapping: A Procedure for Visual Representation and Assessment of Subjective Multiple Group Memberships." *British Journal of Social Psychology* 55 (2016) 613–42.

Stryker, Sheldon, and Richard T. Serpe. "Identity Salience and Psychological Centrality: Equivalent, Overlapping, or Complementary Concepts?" *Social Psychology Quarterly* 57 (1994) 16–35.

Suárez-Ortega, Magdalena. "Performance, Reflexivity, and Learning Through Biographical-Narrative Research." *Qualitative Inquiry* 19 (2013) 189–200.

Swinton, John, and Harriet Mowat. *Practical Theology and Qualitative Research.* 2nd ed. London: SCM, 2016.

Tajfel, Henri. "Experiments in Intergroup Discrimination." *Social Psychology* 223 (1970) 96–103.

———. "Social Identity and Intergroup Behaviour." *Social Science Information* 13 (1974) 65–93.

———, ed. *Differentiation Between Social Groups: Studies in the Social Psychology of Intergroup Relations.* London: Academic, 1979.

Tajfel, Henri, and John C. Turner. "The Social Identity Theory of Intergroup Behavior." In *Political Psychology: Key Readings*, edited by J. T. Jost and J. Sidanius, 276–93. Philadelphia: Psychology Press, 2004.

Toney, Carl N. "The Strong and Weak in Romans 14–15: Ending Divisions and Promoting Additions." PhD diss., Loyola University Chicago, 2007.

Tracy, D. "The Foundations of Practical Theology." In *Practical Theology: The Emerging Field in Theology, Church, and World*, edited by D. S. Browning, 61–82. San Francisco: Harper and Row, 1983.

Tucker, J. Brian. *"Remain in Your Calling": Paul and the Continuation of Social Identities in 1 Corinthians.* Eugene, OR: Wipf & Stock, 2011.

Tucker, J. Brian, and Coleman A. Baker, eds. *T&T Clark Handbook to Social Identity in the New Testament.* London: T&T Clark, 2016.

Turner, John C. "Social Comparison and Social Identity: Some Prospects for Intergroup Behaviour." *European Journal of Social Psychology* 5 (1975) 1–34.

Bibliography

Turner, John C., et al. *Rediscovering the Social Group: A Self-Categorization Theory.* Cambridge: Basil Blackwell, 1987.

Turner, John C., et al. "Self and Collective: Cognition and Social Context." *Personality and Social Psychology Bulletin* 20 (1994) 454–63.

Tusting, Karin. *Congregational Studies in the UK: Christianity in a Post-Christian Context.* New York: Routledge, 2004.

VandenBos, Gary R. *APA Dictionary of Psychology.* 2nd ed. Washington, DC: American Psychological Association, 2015.

Van Dyken, Tamara J. "Worship Wars, Gospel Hymns, and Cultural Engagement in American Evangelicalism, 1890–1940." *Religion and American Culture* 27 (2017) 191–217.

Veling, Terry A. *Practical Theology: On Earth as It Is in Heaven.* Maryknoll, NY: Orbis Books, 2005.

Ward, Mark. "Sermons as Social Interaction: Pulpit Speech, Power, and Gender." *Women and Language* 42 (2019) 285–316.

Ward, Pete. *Introducing Practical Theology: Mission, Ministry, and the Life of the Church.* Grand Rapids: Baker Academic, 2017.

Webster, John. "The Holiness and Love of God." *Scottish Journal of Theology* 57 (2004) 249–68.

Williams, R. R. "Constructing a Calling: The Case of Evangelical Christian International Students in the United States." *Sociology of Religion* 74 (2013) 254–80.

———. "Space for God: Lived Religion at Work, Home, and Play." *Sociology of Religion* 71 (2010) 257–79.

Wuthnow, Robert. "Community Spirit: Small-Town Identities That Bind." In *Small-Town America: Finding Community, Shaping the Future,* edited by Robert Wuthnow, 101–38. Princeton: Princeton University Press, 2013.

Xiao, Sonya Xinyue, et al. "Young Adults' Intergroup Prosocial Behavior and Its Associations with Social Dominance Orientation, Social Identities, Prosocial Moral Obligation, and Belongingness." *Journal of Social and Personal Relationships* 40 (2023) 2809–31.

www.ingramcontent.com/pod-product-compliance
Lightning Source LLC
Chambersburg PA
CBHW052341230426
43664CB00041B/2599